BABE RUTH

His Life and Times

Paul Adomites
Saul Wisnia

Publications International, Ltd.

Paul Adomites is the author of *October's Game* and was a contributing writer to *Treasury of Baseball, Total Baseball,* and *Encyclopedia of Baseball Team Histories.* He served as Publications Director for the Society of American Baseball Research (SABR), founded and edited *The SABR Review of Books,* and its successor, *The Cooperstown Review.* He is a frequent sports contributor to *Pirates Magazine* and *In Pittsburgh.* (Chapters 1, 2, 5, and 6)

Saul Wisnia is a sportswriter for the *Washington Post* and was a contributing writer to *Treasury of Baseball.* He has written for the *Boston Globe* and the *Boston Red Sox Program Magazine,* and was editor of the *Boston Bruins* fan magazine. He has also served as archivist for the Sports Museum of New England and co-hosted a weekly Boston sports radio talk show. (Chapters 3, 4, 7, and 8)

Special thanks to Mark Rucker and Transcendental Graphics, and to Debbie Goodsite and staff at the Bettmann Archive, for their help in tracking rare Babe Ruth photography.

ISBN: 0-7853-1330-3

Library of Congress Catalog Card Number: 95-67739

CONT

1895-1948

The Bambino: Legacy of a Legend

"It wasn't just that he hit more home runs than anybody else, he hit them better, higher, farther, with more theatrical timing and a more flamboyant flourish. Nobody could strike out like Babe Ruth. Nobody circled the bases with the same pigeon-toed, mincing majesty."

—**Red Smith, sports columnist**

THE BAMBINO: LEGACY OF A LEGEND

Previous page: Like a schoolboy at recess, the Babe delights in a chase with his favorite fans.

*I*n the Baltimore Harbor District, you might choose to seek out a particularly humble-looking structure located at 216 Emory Street. This is the building in which Babe Ruth was born. At one time, it was his mother's parents' home; it is now the Babe Ruth Museum. You can stand at the roped-off doorway and peer into the second floor street-side room and look at the bed where Babe Ruth made his entrance into this world. As you stand there, you have to wonder what that moment was like a century ago when midwife Minnie Graf slapped the newborn George Ruth on his rump. Was his first cry the choked, mewling squawl every parent knows? Or did a roar of Ruthian proportions bellow forth from those tiny lungs as the Babe breathed his first air? The fact that we can ask that question at all says a great deal about Babe Ruth.

The genesis of a legend. The birthplace of Babe Ruth is now a museum honoring him.

In all of baseball history, there has never been anyone like Babe Ruth. Yes, he was an athlete of imposing skills, but we have had plenty of those. He was a grand performer in the arena of professional sports, but there seems to be a new one of those every weekend. He forever changed the way baseball was played, inventing the home run as an offensive weapon, but some authorities will tell you that if it hadn't been Ruth, it would have been someone else. What made him so unique and endearing was the way all these things were wrapped up in one boyish, fun-loving package.

Baby George's birth certificate.

He arrived in New York City, the nation's noisiest and busiest town as the Roaring Twenties started. Lest we forget, he was a major force in making them roar. No other city on the continent could have contained him. No other place and no other time could have satisfied his exorbitant and exuberant tastes. Along with his immense accomplishments on the field and outrageous escapades off it, he was immensely lovable in everything he did.

Because of his unmistakable face and form, Ruth was more than just a great athlete and world-renowned character. He was a presence. He was instantly recognizable (who besides his own father ever really looked like Babe Ruth?), and he made you think of everyone's fun-loving, favorite uncle. Biographer Lawrence Ritter described the impact he had on people in the stands. "On a baseball field he was, for almost twenty years, the center of attention no matter what he was doing: from the time he first stepped out of the dugout for batting or fielding practice, hours before a game was scheduled to begin, until the last out in the ninth inning, most of the audience seemed mesmerized by his presence. Fans in the box seats and bleachers alike, at home or away, spent most of their time watching his every move."

Ruth defined a uniquely American style of folk hero: superior prowess at his sport, riding along with appetites as gigantic as his gargantuan home runs, an intense and abiding love of children, and a thoroughly irrepressible sense of fun. The insatiable hunger of Americans for

The Babe and his first wife, Helen.

more—more life, more fun, more laughter, more money—has as its eternal icon Babe Ruth. Unlike many figures held in such esteem, it wasn't after his death that people looked up and noticed what a grand and charming character he was. (In fact, the tolerant and charitable attitude of the sportswriters of his time meant that many great stories of Ruthian adventure were never told.) He was a legend while he lived because he lived his life as a legend. The coined adjective "Ruthian" is used to describe events of stunning and awesome effect, like the Babe's homers, or his sandwiches. Problem was, the word is absurd hyperbole if you try to apply it to anything done by anybody but Babe Ruth.

Everyone wanted a picture with the Bambino. Here, President Warren G. Harding hams it up.

Of course, there was that wink. As broad as his smile and just as captivating, Babe Ruth's wink let everybody know that we were all in on the same joke. With that gesture, he told you life was sheer, exultant joy. It also told you he knew he was not fooling anybody; he didn't have to. He'd wink at folks in the stands, at girls on the street, even at the opposing third baseman when he circled the bags after knocking the stuffing out of an unsuspecting baseball, again. "This is easy," the winking Babe was saying. "This is fun."

Babe Ruth loved people, but he never learned the knack of remembering their names. Sometimes he'd call them "kid" or even more strangely, "keed," an odd way to make a word that designates a child sound even more diminutive. Because Ruth remained a "keed" nearly his whole life, that's what everyone else was to him.

The big kid had a special spot in his heart for the little kids.

Baseball history is teeming with grand, goofy, and wiseacre nicknames. It seems only fitting that the best ballplayer of all time had the best one. No nickname ever fit a player more perfectly. The Babe. The handle tossed at

him by the veterans on Jack Dunn's 1914 minor league Baltimore Orioles stuck like glue and has stayed forever.

During the peak of his career, nobody was photographed more often. One reason for that is he was impossible to miss. Another reason, probably more accurate than the first, is that everyone wanted that personal connection with him. Only the president of the United States had his name in print more than Babe Ruth. With his unforgettable grin, Ruth was also one of the first people to rake in millions for advertising endorsements. However, before he hooked up with business manager Christy Walsh, Ruth was, not surprisingly, just about giving away his name and likeness for advertising use. His name and reputation were spread far and wide; there was virtually no one who didn't know of the Babe. The tale is told that during World War II, when American and Japanese soldiers got close enough during battle to engage in some trash talking, the Yanks would shout "To Hell with the Emperor!" and the Japanese would yell back "To Hell with Babe Ruth!"

Since Babe Ruth's day, there have been other "superstars" in American culture, individuals whose talent and captivating style touch something important enough in us for us to idolize and adore them. Yet, it seems most fall victim to the adulation. They change from glorious figures blessed with great ability to pouty, fallen stars. Ruth lived a life of unquenchable thirsts and insatiable passions, and he never seemed to change. The kid in him never went away.

The hugely familiar face of Babe Ruth shines out from thousands of photographs as a grinning, joyful, oversize child. The best ones show him in the middle of a swarm

His familiar face glows above a sea of adoring fans.

Eleanor Gehrig described the Babe as "a huge man and a small child combined in one runaway personality." Whether he was lending his name to a charitable cause or in the thick of a pennant race, the Babe always found the humor in life around him.

Babe Ruth: His Life and Times

of admiring youngsters, where the pleasure on his face is absolutely sure and overwhelmingly honest. Babe Ruth really was a child in his innocent embrace of life and his complete lack of guile. One of the Xaverian brothers who taught him, Brother Gilbert, said of him that he always "looked out on the world with the grave and solemn wonder of a child." Ruth was truly the all-American boy, not like we've seen in idealized portraits of do-gooders with perfect hair and haughty principles, but in the way a real boy really behaves: sometimes impish, sometimes sweet,

sometimes rude, but always full of life, always testing the limits. Climbing higher, driving faster, ceaselessly pushing for more.

Ruth's childlike consistency of character throughout his life could have come about because his own childhood was difficult. It certainly was not typical. All but abandoned by his parents because their family business forced them to work long, long hours, his first mentors were the street toughs of the Baltimore piers. Removed from his parents' care when he wasn't yet eight years old, he was sent to St. Mary's, a walled boarding school where the 850 boys in attendance called themselves "the inmates." He came to maturity in a world of ragtag boys, supervised by the intimidating (though loving) presence of the Brothers of the Congregation of St. Francis Xavier, or Xaverians. The staunch father figure of Brother Matthias made sure he learned his alphabet and catechism, but Matthias also was his baseball coach. It was on the field that Ruth's irrepressible spirit was encouraged. It is well-known that the

best way to teach children self-esteem is to find something they are good at and push them for further excellence. That's exactly what Brother Matthias did for Ruth. The big kid's talent was baseball. His inborn physical ability was nurtured, and with hours of hard work, his skills perfected.

Ruth's deep concern for kids was evident early in his life. On the playing fields of St. Mary's, he took special interest in the younger boys. On cold days he could be found helping the little ones to stay warm, blowing on their hands, rubbing their tiny fingers in his oversize paws. He loved to treat them to candy he bought with the credits he earned from the candy store for his vocational duty. It wasn't that he was trying to buy love or affection. Sharing the candy was sharing the joy.

The first time he asked Dunn for free passes to an Oriole game, the manager was suspicious. "Who are they for?" he asked. "Some friends of mine," Ruth answered ambiguously. The nervous Dunn watched carefully until he saw Ruth escorting in six boys from St. Mary's into the stands. When he received his first paycheck—$50—as a professional ballplayer, he rushed out and bought a bicycle. According to biographer Robert Creamer, while the Babe was working on his autobiography with writer Bob Considine the year before he died, Ruth was firm that the book not mention he had lost a lot of money while gambling in Cuba. "It wouldn't be good for the kids," he explained. The last few years of his life he was active in the Ford Junior Legion baseball program. One teammate called him "a humanitarian beyond belief."

The Maharajah of Mash signs autographs and jokes with those he cherished most. No one was ever turned away.

The legend in motion. He soared higher than most dare to dream.

His excellent hand-eye coordination made the Babe a skilled hunter, too.

Ruth lived bigger than life. His huge appetites were the stuff of legend. Never having been trained in the finer graces of life, he could be crude. A Ruthian belch was always good for an appreciative laugh. While people certainly could get mad at the Babe, one would be hard-pressed to find a soul who didn't like him. Ruth loved being loved.

His excesses—food, drink, and anything else that he considered fun—were sometimes embarrassing. At an off-season baseball dinner before the 1923 season, New York State Senator (and later Mayor) Jimmy Walker gave Babe a noisy and publicized dressing down. He called Ruth a "great fool" for his poor training habits, his overweight physique, and rowdy behavior. The cut that made the deepest wound—and may really have been the impetus for the Babe to get himself in shape and begin a run of hitting more than 40 homers in nine out of 10 years—was Walker's next comment: "You're letting down the kids of America."

On at least one occasion, his excesses were dangerous. A particularly Ruthian bout of overindulgence had him rushed to the hospital in 1925. They called it "The Bellyache Heard 'Round the World." Ruth spent seven weeks in the hospital and had to pay a huge fine and apologize to his teammates before Manager Miller Huggins would let him play again.

Unfortunately, the most common motion pictures of

Take a bow, Bambino.

Ruth, taken late in his career, have given many people the false notion that Babe was always a fat man, nearly comic in his gait. The two theatrical films made of his career overstate that fact substantially. The truth is, while Ruth's body was hardly the prototype for a Charles Atlas ad, when he came into the majors at age 19, he was tall and muscular but not large. He sucked up food the way he sucked up the adoration of the fans: heartily. That lifestyle added a few pounds. However, for most of the years he spent on the field he was paunchy but hardly obese. (It would have been amazing if a man with Ruth's taste for beer and chow didn't have a little extra around his gut.) In truth, he was an excellent baserunner (despite a legendary gaffe to end the 1926 World Series) and not slow at all. Five times he stole more than 10 bases in a season. He even stole home 10 times in his career; only two people who have played in the past 50 years have accomplished that feat more often.

In his chosen world, Babe Ruth was a genius. His place as the greatest baseball player of all time is unassailable. While famous sportswriter Bob Broeg may have said, "Trying to capture Babe Ruth with cold statistics would be like trying to keep up with him on a night out," it doesn't matter how you slice it, the Babe comes out way ahead of whoever's second. Lifetime, he is second in home runs (although no one ever hit homers with greater frequency), on-base percentage, runs batted in, and runs scored. He ranks first in walks and slugging average, third in extra base hits, fifth in total bases, and ninth in batting average. He broke the lifetime

At times, Babe found life's greatest pleasures to also be the simplest.

home run record in 1921, and it wasn't surpassed for some 53 years. If Ruth had batted as often as Henry Aaron did and maintained his lifetime home run percentage, he would have out-homered Hank by 299 circuit clouts. In the new stats of lifetime batting runs and batting wins, no one is even close to him. There is nothing "cold" about those numbers.

Babe and Claire Ruth with their daughters, Dorothy and Julia

The Sultan's rich career singles him out as the definitive player.

His single-season accomplishments may be even more amazing. For an astounding number of times, he led his league in an offensive category. A dozen times he hit more homers than anyone else, eight times he scored more runs, six times he drove in more than anyone else, 11 times he received more walks than anyone else in the league, and 13 times he had the highest slugging average. He won only one batting title but was second or third five times. Only one player ever scored more runs in a season; only one hit more homers. Ruth holds the top three season marks for home run percentage and the record for single-season total bases and walks. Of the top nine slugging years, six belong to Babe; five of the top on-base percentage seasons are his, as well.

When you combine all the stats to get "the one big number" (something today's stat folks love to do), his "Total Baseball Ranking" is 122½. Second best is Nap Lajoie, falling into place nearly 30 points behind.

If you hear someone claim that despite that staggering evidence, Aaron, Wagner, Cobb, or Lajoie were "really" better, ask this question: How many games did they pitch and win in the big

leagues? Ruth won 94. (Nine major league teams began the 1994 season without a 94-game winner on their staffs—not including the expansion teams.) Ruth was also undefeated in three World Series starts. For four years he was considered the best left-hander in the major leagues.

Manager Joe McCarthy sits with superstars Babe and Lou Gehrig. After the Babe changed the game, the trailblazer would pass the flame.

The final proof of Ruth's status as the best ever has to do with the nature of the game itself. When baseball found itself frightened and confused by the "Black Sox" scandal and the accidental yet fatal beaning of Ray Chapman, Ruth came along and brought the big swing and the home run into the game. Previously, this style of game was considered rather entertaining but hardly a reliable amusement. Since Babe blazed the trail, the game has never been the same.

Financially speaking, he also left an indelible mark. While he was swatting the ball out of every park in existence, he forever changed the economic structure of the game. Professional athletes, always acknowledged and revered, became wealthy because of Ruth's impact on baseball's pay scales.

Perhaps Waite Hoyt summed it up best when he said, "Every big league player and his wife should teach their children to pray, 'God bless Mommy, God bless Daddy, God bless Babe Ruth.'"

Perhaps the Babe summed it up best when he said: "Baseball was, is, and always will be to me the best game in the world."

1895-1914

Humble Beginnings: The Talented Truant

"What I am, what I have, what I am going to leave behind me— all this I owe to the game of baseball, without which I would have come out of St. Mary's Industrial School in Baltimore a tailor, and a pretty bad one at that."

—Babe Ruth, comment made during the making of *The Babe Ruth Story*, released in 1948

HUMBLE BEGINNINGS: THE TALENTED TRUANT

Previous page: Babe Ruth signs his first professional contract.

No one knew that this tiny baby would someday be baseball's greatest slugger. Young George Ruth Jr. does what he would do many times later in life as he poses for the camera.

On February 6, 1895, George Ruth Jr. came into this world, the first of eight children born to George Ruth Sr. and Kate Schamberger Ruth. To anyone who has ever seen a picture of his grown son, the Babe's father had strikingly similar features: round face with a wide nose and mouth. Babe's mother was a tiny woman, standing only 4'10". She was just 19 years old when Babe was born and would not live to see 36. Of the seven other children she gave birth to (three boys plus George, including one set of twins, and four girls, also with one set of twins), she would outlive all of them except Babe and his sister Mary, nicknamed Mamie by her older brother.

The Ruth family had a tough life. George Sr., after trying his hand at several businesses (including his father's somewhat questionable lightning rod operation), was a saloonkeeper. According to Ruth biographer Marshall Smelser, peddling food and drinks was a highly competitive enterprise in Baltimore at that time. Smelser says there were "licensed sellers of legal beverages for each 105 Baltimoreans, the highest known ratio in the country." In addition, the economic panic of 1893, which shut the doors of more than 500 banks and 15,000 businesses across the nation, had thrown many locals out of work, making it even harder to earn a living owning a saloon.

George and Kate did the only thing they could: work harder. They kept the bar open longer hours so as not to miss any prospective customers. Work weeks that consisted of 100 hours of labor were the rule. Their young son was largely left to fend for himself.

The youngster found his fun in the rough and tumble world of the Baltimore harbor, where he was a quick study. He learned the street skills of rowdiness and petty larceny, running and romping with older boys, breaking windows, engaging in other high-spirited (but largely harmless) hijinks. It would be hard to claim that

Ruth was truly a delinquent. Of course he was full of boyish pranks, and the older boys he hung out with weren't good influences. He had a taste for chewing tobacco by the time he reached seven. His problem was that he was a real boy without a real family to keep him in line and teach him how to behave. One of his favorite tricks was to swipe money from the cash drawer at the family bar and use it to treat the neighborhood kids to ice cream. He grew fast, in body and in the ways of the world. The one thing he couldn't stomach was school. Truancy was his way of life.

The public schools at the time were awful places to be. They were often over-crowded, dirty, and run by teachers who weren't good enough to find work at the higher-paying private schools. Classrooms were no fun, especially for an energetic young lad like George, with his fondness for street-style rowdy behavior. His parents, committed by necessity to long work hours and debilitated by his mother's increasingly frail condition, couldn't pull in the reins on this youngster. Ruth didn't

Taken at a family picnic around 1896, this is the only known photograph of Babe Ruth with his mother and father. Kate Schamberger Ruth is seen (first row, far left) *turning George Jr.'s head to the camera. George Sr., also in the first row, is wearing a bow tie and holding a glass of beer and a long-stemmed pipe.*

Wearing a cap, the seven-year-old Ruth hooks arms with a pal from St. Mary's. Life inside the walls of the Industrial School provided a regimented routine for the boys.

seem to understand his family's financial plight or his mother's ill health. Years later he said, "I think my mother hated me."

So in 1902, Ruth's father, mother, and a Justice of the Peace filed the form that legally labeled the seven-year-old George Ruth Jr. "incorrigible and vicious . . . beyond the control" of his parents. He was committed to the St. Mary's Industrial School for Boys and legally removed from his parents' care, becoming a ward of the Xaverian Brothers who operated the school. On Friday, June 13, George Ruth Sr. took his tearful son by the hand and delivered him to St. Mary's. The youngster begged to return home with his father and probably vowed by all he knew as holy to mend his ways. His tears had no effect; his rowdiness and truancy had cost him. George Ruth Jr. would spend most of his next 12 years inside the walls of St. Mary's. When he left for good, it would be because he had signed a professional baseball contract.

St. Mary's, located a few miles outside downtown Baltimore, consisted of six gray buildings on several acres with a large open space that fit two ballfields, the Big Yard

The Juniors' building at St. Mary's as it appeared in 1913. Located only four miles southwest of downtown Baltimore, the peaceful locale provided by the Xaverian Brothers was quite a contrast to city life.

and the Little Yard. Although it was surrounded by a wooden fence, and the boys there called themselves "inmates," it was less a prison than some have said. (St. Mary's did become a true reformatory in the 1930s.) Some of the more than 800 students, like George, had been committed there by the courts for minor offenses. The remainder

Physical activity played an important role in the daily schedule of the boy's of St. Mary's. It was on these grounds of the Big Yard and the Little Yard that the Babe developed his love for the game.

of the student population was comprised of others who were true delinquents, others who were orphans (this is how the "Orphaned Ruth" myth came about), and still others who were actually boarders whose attendance was paid for by their parents. The Brothers of the Order of St. Francis Xavier who ran the school, however, made no distinction. To the Brothers they were all the same: boys without families. All were there to benefit from the discipline, activity, education, and training made available. The Brothers were strict, but they were fair. Punishment was seldom corporal. The usual penalty for bad behavior by any of the boys was the withholding of some privilege. One of the most effective punishments (as Ruth would find out later) was being forbidden from taking part in the ballgames. Desertions from the school were actually quite rare. The boys were expected to stay there until they turned 21.

The core mission of the Xaverian Brothers was (and still is) working with disadvantaged youth, usually in cities. What they taught the wild young Ruth changed him forever. The Brothers operated with a simple premise: Idleness breeds trouble.

So the boys were kept busy on a rigorous schedule that seldom varied. School, training, prayer, work, and play were all parts of the minute-by-minute daily routine.

Smelser's description of a typical day there: "Up at six to wash and dress for Mass and breakfast. . . . Classes—academic or vocational—from breakfast until 10 in the morning. Recess from 10 to 10:30. School or work from 10:30 to 11:30. Din-

The Brothers at St. Mary's were concerned with providing their charges with a trade that would enable them to earn a wage after leaving the safety of the school's walls. They trained the boys in a variety of skills, including shirtmaking and typesetting.

ner and free time from 11:30 to 1:30. School again until 3:15, after which [time] there was a class in Catholic doctrine, required of Catholics only. From then until supper at six the boys played, the small boys in the Little Yard, and the boys of fifteen or older in the Big Yard." After supper the boys were supposed to read in bed from 7:30 until lights out 45 minutes later.

The Brother who stood largest in the young Ruth's life (and in the sight of everyone there) was Brother Matthias. Matthias was well-equipped for his duties as prefect of discipline and assistant to Brother Herman, director of athletics. A 6'6" pear-shaped giant who weighed around 250 pounds, Brother Matthias was quietly stolid, but his commanding physical presence was enough to quell schoolyard mutinies without saying a word.

Brother Matthias became teacher, mentor, coach, and friend to the young truant. This bond, forged early on, stayed with Ruth his entire life. In 1947, when he was writing his autobiography with Bob Considine, Ruth said, "It was at St. Mary's that I met and learned to love the greatest man I've ever known. His name was Brother Matthias. He was the father I needed. He taught me to read and write—and he taught me the difference between right and wrong."

George Ruth would be an "inmate" of St. Mary's for seven and a half of the next dozen years. He was released to his parents on several occasions. However, regular school still wasn't to his liking, and before long he'd be carted back to the Brothers by the truant officers. For 10 years the young Ruth could visit his family only for the holidays; nearly every weekend, though, his mother and sister Mamie came to visit him. Then, around 1910, his mother died. From that point until he left the school to become a baseball player, he never had another visitor. He felt the snub keenly. "I guess I'm too ugly," he told a friend, in a totally unRuthian display of self-deprecation.

Several years after his time at St. Mary's, a young Ruth strikes a reflective pose.

Each boy under the supervision of the Xaverian Brothers was allowed to choose a trade. From a long list that included printer, shoemaker, electrician, carpenter, florist, and launderer, Ruth elected to learn how to sew shirts. Most of the shirts were made for the boys at the school to wear; some were sold to outside vendors. Each boy was paid a small amount for the shirts he made. Ruth routinely spent all his at the candy store and spread his sweet earnings among the smaller kids.

George's concern for the young lads at the school was heartfelt and natural. On chilly days in the yard, he was seen blowing on the hands of cold youngsters to warm them. Throughout his life, Ruth never outgrew his love for children, perhaps because he never really outgrew being a kid himself.

Although other sports were played in the recreational areas at St. Mary's, baseball was a favorite. The teams were quite competitive with each other. Sometimes the Xaverian Brothers would organize a game with other local teams.

One of many championships teams the future-great Ruth would be a part of. Standing at the top left, the Babe holds his catchers' mask in one hand. Since there were no left-handed mitts available, he would have to make do with a right-handed glove.

Many youngsters honed their athletic skills while thriving under the tutelage of the Brothers.

Young George had certain innate abilities. For example, with his natural superiority in hand-eye coordination, the youngster was a superb shirtmaker. According to Smelser, he "claimed he could sew a shirt in less than a quarter of an hour," which prompted the biographer to suggest, "If he had stayed with his trade, he could have made as much as $20 a week." Before long $20 would be the tip Babe Ruth left for breakfast.

Despite the considerable promise he showed as a shirtmaker, it was on the ballfield that Ruth truly excelled. Sports were a vital part of life at St. Mary's, and although there were seven team sports played, baseball was the game of choice. One of the Xaverian Brothers was quoted as saying, "Play is the eighth sacrament." Baseball tournaments between different dormitories and trade groups went on as long as the weather would permit. Large for his age, and with his remarkable athletic gifts, Ruth was playing with the 12-year-olds by the time he was eight or nine, with the 16-year-olds when he was just 12. He was on the varsity, playing with men as old as 20, at the tender age of 16.

Ruth learned through long hours of practice. The sessions of fungo catching were usually hosted by the imposing Brother Matthias, who would wear a glove on his left hand, toss the ball out of it, and slug a fly with the bat in his right hand. Some say the huge Matthias had

once injured a boy when he swung the bat with both hands. "He was a great hitter," Ruth later remembered.

Matthias also taught Ruth how to run: pigeon-toed. The theory is that running that way makes you faster, because you can push off with all five toes. It seemed to work for the gangly kid. Ruth's famous pigeon-toe trot became part of his legend.

Young George was capable of any position, even though his lefthandedness meant he had to play with a righthander's glove. His chosen position was catcher, from where he demonstrated a great arm. One fellow student described in later years how Ruth dealt with attempted base stealers from behind the plate: "He would catch the ball in the glove on his left hand, toss the ball straight up, drop the mitt on the ground, catch the ball again in his bare left hand and throw." In retrospect, it seems unlikely that this kind of performance was standard operating procedure for Ruth, although the teammate's description proved he could have done it when he chose. It's more likely

There is some speculation on just how the young Babe (top row, center) handled his tasks as catcher without the proper equipment. Regardless of how he did it, he did it well.

that he did what lefthanders forced to deal with righthanded gloves have done since baseball gloves were invented: he simply wore the mitt designed for the left hand on his right hand. Some photographs that were taken while he was at St. Mary's indicate that was his style.

Ruth said himself that hitting came naturally to him, but it was the tutelage of Brother Matthias that gave him the discipline to become a good fielder as well. Ruth was the star catcher for the Red Sox, one of St. Mary's intramural teams (all were named after major league nines), when he first became a pitcher.

There are two stories of how he took the mound for the first time. In one, the Red Sox hurler, the delightfully named Congo Kirby, lost his baseball privileges

A fire would destroy part of St. Mary's in April 1919. Never forgetting the impact of the Brothers on his life, Babe rose to the occasion when a fundraiser was organized, donating one-fifth of his salary.

for some misdemeanor, and Ruth asked Brother Matthias if he could take over the pitching duties. In the other, pitcher Kirby was being battered around in one game, and Ruth found it terribly amusing. In the eternal style of parents and teachers throughout the ages, Brother Matthias chided the wisecracking youth with, "If you know so much about pitching, why not do it yourself?" A superstar hurler was born.

Ruth's performances on the diamond quickly began to attract notice. In 1912, the St. Mary's newspaper reported a game in which the 17-year-old batted leadoff and rapped a homer, a triple, and a double. In the same game, he played third base, caught, and even pitched, fanning six batters.

By the summer of the following year, the walls of St. Mary's were too small for his prodigious talent. As a pitcher that season he was undefeated. When he wasn't pitching, he was the catcher. He batted .537. In one intramural game he struck out 22 batters. Newspaper sources appear to indicate that the 18-year-old Ruth was being allowed to play for semipro teams in the area.

A local article referred to a pitcher for the St. Patrick's Catholic Club named "Roth," bestowing the nickname "the speed boy," for Ruth's fastball was noteworthy. At 6'2" and 150 pounds, George had the size to deliver the smoke. While newspaper reports from this time are a bit sketchy, Ruth does show up in the boxscore for another semipro team, the Bayonnes, that year.

In a February 1918 interview in *Baseball Magazine*, the then 24-year-old Ruth reminisced about his ballplaying days at school. "I wasn't a pitcher in those days until I was pretty nearly through my course. My main job was catching. . . . I used to hit .450 and .500. I kept track one season and found that I made over 60 home runs. The last two years I pitched and got along pretty well, but I never lost my taste for hitting and don't expect to." The Ruth being interviewed had hit just nine major league home runs at the time; he was strictly a pitcher. His comments about loving hitting—even mentioning the magical 60-homer number, which no one in baseball history had ever hit half of, and which even Ruth wouldn't reach for nearly 10 more years—seem strangely prophetic.

The Xaverian Brothers also ran a boys' college, Mount St. Joseph's, not far from St. Mary's. There was good-natured competition between the two schools. The Industrial School boys took the collegians for snobs; the college kids saw their counterparts as ruffians. Mount St. Joseph's was boasting of their own star pitcher at the time, a young man named Bill Morrisette, who in the 1913 season used his spitball to throw a no-hitter, a one-hitter, a three-hitter, and a five-hitter against competition such as Holy Cross, Georgetown, and Bucknell. (Morrisette would go on to a 13-game major league career.) As part of

His familiar features now apparent, Babe's talents flourished on the ball field. He had continued to develop as an athlete and would often play on teams with older players.

The Baltimore Orioles of the International League in 1914. George Ruth (far right) became one of Jack Dunn's hand-picked prospects for the team.

Babe could be devastating on the mound. As a young hurler, some local papers dubbed him "the speed boy."

the commencement day festivities for Mount St. Joseph's, the Brothers cooked up a plan to have Ruth pitch against Morrisette.

For the first time anyone knows, the man who would be the mighty Babe Ruth was noticeably frightened by the pressure of this upcoming challenge. His fear overtook him, and 10 days before the game, he ran away from St. Mary's, the first time he had left in two years. The boys at the school were aghast. The gossip spread concerning his disappearance. He was gone for two days before being corralled by the school's probation officer and night watchman, who found him in his old haunts on the piers. The official word that he had returned voluntarily was treated with scorn by the other boys. Ruth received a severe punishment for his desertion. For five days, he was forbidden to play ball, and instead he had to "stand guard" on the road between the Big Yard and the Little Yard and watch the others. When Ruth's penance had been paid, Brother Matthias reminded him the big game was just two days away and encouraged him to start throwing again immediately.

The precise details of the challenge contest were never recorded. One thing stands out crystal clear, however. Ruth dominated, striking out at least 14 of the Mount St. Joseph's players and allowing no runs. Morrisette was racked for six runs, maybe more.

At the time, Baltimore had a very successful minor league team, the Orioles, owned by a former big league player named Jack Dunn. He became the Orioles manager in 1907, and by 1910 he owned the team. (Ironically, Baltimore had no major league team because the Orioles had moved to New York in 1903 to become the Highlanders, later the Yankees, as part of the settlement between the old National and new American Leagues.) Dunn had a keen eye for baseball talent and was a shrewd businessman. While his team was a success on the field and at the box office, his greatest source of income came from selling his players to the majors. Certainly Dunn, the savvy operator that he was, had heard of "the speed boy" playing at the Industrial School. His ears were open to men like Mount St. Joseph's Brother Gilbert; to Joe Engel, a former major league pitcher and alumnus of Brother Gilbert's school; and, according to Smelser, to "assorted Baltimore bartenders [including] George Herman Ruth Sr."

Although he had already endured many hardships in his life, the Babe kept his sense of humor. While not everyone appreciated his jokes, he was often horsing around.

Although he missed the Morrisette/Ruth matchup, Brother Gilbert had seen two typical Ruthian performances in September 1913. In one, when Ruth came to bat the first time, the opposing rightfielder moved all the way from his normal position in the Big Yard to near second base in the Little Yard, 280 feet away from Ruth's bat. (The boys in the Little Yard stopped play; they knew who was up.) George didn't disappoint, slugging the ball off the Little Yard's farthest fence, quite a poke with the dead ball of the day. In another game attended by Brother Gilbert, Ruth belted a pair of homers.

There was no mistaking the fact that the young man named Ruth was something special on a baseball diamond. He already possessed the athlete's calm and keen grace. He was relaxed and poised, both at the bat and on the mound. Perhaps more importantly, the Brothers who taught him thought highly of his character. The wild tobacco-chewing urchin of the docks who had been brought there 12 years earlier was now a responsible young man. While he had grown physically and mentally, his fun-loving nature was still intact.

Dunn, who had recently signed Morrisette, was invited to St. Mary's to give the youth a tryout. Arriving with Brother Gilbert and Yankee infielder Fritz Maisel on February 14, 1914, Dunn was introduced to Ruth's mentor, Brother Matthias.

Dunn explained why he was there. The Brother offered one terse comment, "Ruth can hit." Then Dunn asked, "Can he pitch?" "Sure, he can do anything," the king-size Brother replied. No assessment ever contained truer words. After half an hour of throwing the ball around, Dunn decided to sign Ruth on the spot. Because Ruth was still the legal ward of the school's head, Brother Paul, Dunn had to assume guardianship in order to sign him, but this was a common practice used by the Brothers to "graduate" their boys to full-time employment.

George Herman Ruth Jr. (he had taken Herman as his Confirmation name, in honor of one of the Brothers at St. Mary's and because it was his father's middle name) was signed to play for Dunn's Baltimore Orioles for the sum of $100 per month—$600 for the full season. For the young man, whose previous experience with money was change he pilfered from the family till or "candy credits" he earned by sewing shirts, this must have seemed a king's ransom! By the time Dunn and Ruth left Brother Paul's office after the signing, word had already spread. A cluster of St. Mary's "inmates" were waiting outside. Someone was heard to say, "There goes our ball club."

Two weeks later, Ruth visited with his father in the family home above the saloon, for his final weekend in Baltimore. He had been in-

Brother Matthias was a towering influence in the lives of many of the young residents at St. Mary's. His most famous student, however, thought of him as a father figure and remembered the kind teacher for the rest of his life.

structed to report to the Keenan Hotel on Monday afternoon, March 2. It was from this point that he was to join up with a group of pitchers and catchers and head south to the Oriole spring training camp in Fayetteville, North Carolina. How excited and nervous he must have been.

Baltimore gave the Babe a noisy sendoff. Between Sunday and Monday, a foot of snow fell. Gale-force winds blew the roofs off houses and even toppled a church steeple. Not even the worst winter storm in 25 years could keep the youngster from making his way to the hotel on Monday. The train, remarkably, left for Fayetteville on time that evening, with Ruth and about a dozen others aboard. Among those who were travelling were Bill Morrisette, another young Baltimore player by the name of Allen Russell, and a left-handed pitcher named Klingelhoefer, who had been anointed with the baseball-perfect nickname of "Smoke."

George Ruth Jr. had never been on a train before. He asked about the purpose of the unusual hammock-like device that hung from the ceiling of his berth. While well-travelled people would know its purpose was to store clothes, the Babe had no clue. One of the old-timers told him it was there as a special rest for pitchers' arms. Ruth tried to sleep with his left arm hanging in the thing and wound up with a stiff shoulder for several days.

Ultimately, it didn't matter. While the weather in Fayetteville wasn't blizzard-like, it still wasn't right for playing baseball. Cold, rainy, and windy, it would be a week before the team could practice on the field. In the meantime, they spent a few hours in the local armory, tossing balls around and playing handball.

I 33

BABE RUTH

Hit his first home run in professional baseball, March, 1914. 135 yds. N.W. In this town George Herman Ruth acquired the nickname "Babe."

What a shot that must have been! Some 38 years after the fact, a man who had been batboy for the game persuaded the government of Fayetteville to put up a marker at the spot honoring Babe Ruth's first home run in pro baseball.

The young Ruth was itching to play, but he certainly wasn't bored. Suddenly freed from the protective eyes of the Brothers, he took boyish delight in his exciting new life. He especially loved the elevator, begging the operator to teach him to run it, and riding up and down for hours at a time. On one occasion, he had his head stuck out of the doors when he accidentally engaged the motor, and the elevator began to rise. Only the frightened shouts of nearby teammates saved him from possible decapitation.

He arose early every morning to go down to the train yards and watch the five o'clock steam engine roll through. After his sojourn to the railyards each morning, he was first in line when the hotel kitchen opened for breakfast. Wide-eyed Ruth was amazed and delighted that he could simply sign for the meals and the ball club would pick up the tab. So great was his appetite that it soon became a long-running joke among his mates on the team.

Rookies of the time, particularly those as green as Ruth, were viciously hazed by the team's veterans for any behavior that seemed even somewhat inappropriate (or for no reason at all.) So the kid's huge tastes kept the older pros in stitches and smart comments. The Orioles, incidently, were not a young team; six men on their roster had played in the majors. Five others in this group were more than 30 years old.

The razzing was merciless, until, the story goes, one of the team's coaches admonished the veterans to let up on hassling Ruth, because "he's one of Jack Dunn's babes." In other words, the boss thinks he's something special. The veterans picked up on the term, and a legendary nickname was born; the young Mr. Ruth would never be George again.

The moniker wasn't original at all, of course. At that time, William "Babe" Borton was a major league first baseman, and Charles "Babe" Adams was one of the best pitchers in the National League. Two other "Babes," Danzig and Towne, had previously appeared in the majors.

Somehow, though, this nickname fit Ruth better than anyone could have imagined. The big kid, with his childlike wonder at a world so new to him, his thunderous adolescent appetites for food and baseball, and his fresh-faced, innocent love of life, became the Babe as no other ever would or could.

Soon the weather improved enough for the Orioles to move their workouts outside, but many of Dunn's players were stuck up north by the awful weather and couldn't get to Fayetteville. By March 7, they had 17 men in camp, so they recruited a sportswriter, Roger Pippen (who had been assigned as a protective measure to be Ruth's roommate), to play center field. They finally had a game.

It was in that game that the newly christened Babe Ruth did what he would do over a thousand times more in big league parks, on ballfields, and on sandlots all around the world: He belted a monumental home run. Ruth, playing for the Buzzards against the Sparrows, went two-for-three as the shortstop and pitcher. The home run he unloaded was called "the longest hit ever seen by Fayetteville fans." (The previous longest hit was by Jim Thorpe.) The ball was hit so far into the right-center alley in the Cape Fear Fairgrounds that Bill Morrisette (stationed in right) hadn't even picked up the ball by the time Ruth reached home. Sportswriter Pippen measured the distance: 350 feet. After one week of professional baseball, players were comparing Ruth's swing to that of slugger Joe Jackson, even though Ruth had never seen "Shoeless Joe" play. The next day the *Baltimore Sun* ran a two-

Roger Pippen was a sportswriter-turned-ballplayer. He was assigned to room with the Orioles' new kid and help keep him out of harm's way. Pippen (far right) is pictured here with the Babe many years later.

Although some early observers compared the Babe's swing to that of Shoeless Joe Jackson, Babe and Joe had not yet met.

Babe Ruth: His Life and Times

column headline: "Homer by Ruth Feature of Game." Some 38 years later, a man who had been batboy for the game persuaded the government of Fayetteville to erect a marker at the spot honoring Babe Ruth's first home run in professional baseball, even though the Fairgrounds themselves were long gone.

In intrasquad games involving the entire roster over the next week, Ruth made headlines one way or another nearly every day: impressive strikeouts when he pitched, excellent fielding when he played short, even a surprising drag bunt for a hit. In a March 14 article discussing the Oriole pitchers, the *Sun* said this:

"Ruth Impresses Dunn. George Ruth has impressed Dunn most, and before he was at training camp a week he decided that he will be a regular whether or not he strikes his stride. The Oriole magnate predicts that Ruth will develop into a Rube Waddell, for he possesses every mark of a successful pitcher."

The Waddell comparison is especially intriguing, because that astonishing pitcher's career was drastically shortened by his inability to control his moods and appetites. Babe, of course, would face many of the same difficulties, but with dramatically different results.

Two days later a *Sun* headline read: "Dunn Praises Ruth: Jack Declares He Is the Most Promising Youngster He Ever Had."

Dunn was quoted in the article as calling Babe, "a whale with the willow . . . some of the drives he is making in practice would clear the right field fence at Oriole Park." To his friend Brother Gilbert, Dunn wrote, "Brother, this fellow Ruth is the greatest young ball player who ever reported to a training camp."

It had been only 14 days since Ruth boarded his first train to become a professional baseball player.

Spring training of the era lacked sophisticated techniques and practice drills. The team got in shape by playing as many games as possible. Dunn scheduled games against anyone, from military academies to major-league outfits. March 18, the Babe got his chance to pitch to big league hitters. It wasn't glorious.

Brought in to face the Philadelphia Phillies in the fourth inning, Ruth immediately allowed singles to both Hans Lobert and Fred Luderus, the former a one-time good hitter now past his prime, the latter just an average player. Sherry Magee, winner of the National League batting title in 1910, drew a walk. Pitching sensation Ruth had loaded the bases with nobody out in his first try at major-league hurling. He settled

down enough to make the next hitter pop up, and the following batter rapped an apparent double-play grounder to short. When shortstop Claude Derrick bobbled it, though, a run scored. Another single drove in a second run. No Phillie hit safely against Ruth in the next two innings, although the Babe did allow two more free passes. The Orioles came back to win 4-3.

Ruth got another chance the next day. The Phillies had pounded Oriole pitching to take a 6-0 lead, with four runs already across in the sixth inning and only one out when Ruth was called in to douse the fire. He fanned Henry Matteson and George Paskert to close out the inning, then pitched three more innings and allowed no runs, surrendered only two hits, and struck out three. The Orioles roared back and won 7-6.

Sherry Magee was a talented player who excelled in the dead-ball era. Magee, winner of the 1910 batting title, was the third batter Ruth faced in his first major-league game.

Frank "Home Run" Baker was a member of the "$100,000 Infield" that made up Connie Mack's Philadelphia Athletics.

Babe Ruth: His Life and Times

In his two appearances against big league batters, the 19-year-old Ruth had faced 29 men and allowed just six hits. Dunn moved him into the starting rotation.

Bad weather delayed his first start for six days, but he took the mound in Wilmington, North Carolina, on March 25 against Connie Mack's potent Philadelphia Athletics. The A's were probably the best team in baseball, having won the World Series three of the past four years. Their lineup could have been called the Murderer's Row of its time. The A's had outscored every other team in the AL in 1913 by at least 161 runs. They routinely led the league in batting average, runs, and homers. These were the A's of the fabled "$100,000 Infield," featuring future Hall of Famers Frank "Home Run" Baker and Eddie Collins.

Ruth surrendered 13 hits to the Mackmen but won the game 6-2 with savvy pitching that dodged the bullet with men on base. Home Run Baker found Ruth's pitches to his liking. He slugged four hits and made an out only when his long drive to right was flagged down. Dunn, eager to drum up business, left for Baltimore to promote another exhibition against the Athletics the following Saturday and promised Ruth would pitch again.

Less than four weeks after George Ruth had quietly left his hometown in search of a dream, he returned to quite a surprise. The papers were now calling him Babe, placing his picture in the sports pages, and encouraging the people of Baltimore to come and see him play. Unfortunately, Ruth pitched poorly on wet grounds and lost 12-5.

However, his opponents were sitting up and taking notice. Phillie coach Pat Moran, who later managed the Phils and Reds to pennants, said, "Ruth is a marvel for a kid just breaking in. I predict that within a few years Ruth will be one of the best southpaws in baseball." Athletics second baseman Eddie Collins said, "Ruth is a sure comer. He has the speed and a sharp curve, and believe me, he is steady in the pinches," an obvious reference to the 13-hit, two-run performance. After Ruth topped the Brooklyn Dodgers in another exhibition, Dodger manager Wilbert Robinson predicted, "He will be one of the sensations of the baseball season."

In that game, Ruth belted a long fly to right that only a running catch by 23-year-old Casey Stengel kept from being a hit. Next time Babe came up to bat, Stengel (on his manager's orders) was playing Ruth even deeper, but the Babe, slugging a ball even Stengel couldn't catch, took it for a triple. Stengel's comment on Ruth's pitching: "He had good stuff, a good fastball, a fine curve—a dipsy-do that made you think a little."

Spring training was winding down, but the Baltimore weather wasn't getting more springlike. Dunn was scheduling games against big league opponents (and having many rained out) for two reasons. One reason was the bigger paydays: More fans would come to see the major leaguers. The other was an attempt to forestall a more serious threat: the Federal League.

Since the American League Baltimore Orioles had moved to New York 11 years earlier, the fans

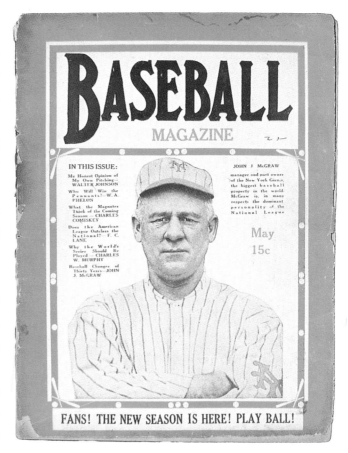

John McGraw was known as a feisty player. Before Ruth became dominant, McGraw was one of the top drawing names in baseball.

of Baltimore had been without major league baseball, and they didn't like it. This situation set particularly poorly with them since their Orioles of the 1890s had been a legendary bunch of snarling, scrapping winners. In 1914, however, a new major league, the Federal League, was starting up, and they had a team in Baltimore, headed by Ned Hanlon, who had managed the old Orioles. The Terrapins, or "Baltfeds," were garnering all the headlines on the Baltimore sports pages.

Dunn scheduled a three-game series against the Giants of John McGraw. McGraw, who had been one of the feistiest of Hanlon's remarkably feisty Orioles, was sure to draw a large crowd. The first day they did. Something very magical happened for the Babe in this outing. He wasn't in the game until late in the ninth inning. With a 2-1 Baltimore lead, Ruth was sent in as a replacement for the first baseman. The infielder had to be dismissed from his post when he lost a tooth and split a lip after he took a shot in the mouth with a batted ball. The tension had been building in the

Babe Adams was one of the best pitchers in the National League

toughly contested match. When a ground ball was fielded and thrown to Ruth at first for the final out, the jubilant youngster, thrilled at the victory over the mighty McGraw Giants, gave out a shout of joy, threw the ball into the stands, and ran down the foul line, encouraging the cheers of the fans. The Babe forged a bond with the fans that would stay with him from that point on.

The Giants won the next day, to a much smaller crowd. The third game coincided with the Terrapin's home opener. The Terrapins drew 28,000 fans; the Orioles about a 1,000. Ruth pitched and lost.

Just as the skies had parted and let go with a mighty snowfall the day Ruth left Baltimore, the miserable weather healed as if by divine intervention on April 22. It was that day that Ruth was scheduled to start the second game of the regular season against the Buffalo Bisons. Although the temperature was in

the 40s in the morning, by noon it was past 70 degrees. By game time it was a luscious 83.

Babe Herman, who began his pro career in 1926, shared the famous moniker with Ruth.

Ruth's nervousness was evident in the first inning he pitched. Ernest J. Lanigan, one of the era's most famous sportswriters, offered this terse description. "Vaughn was thrown out by Ball; McCarthy walked and took second on a wild pitch; Murray flied to Cree; Ruth and Gleichman got mixed up on Houser's pop fly, the ball dropping safely for a hit and McCarthy taking third; Houser stole second; Jackson was hit by a pitched ball, filling the bases; Roach was thrown out [on a spectacular play] by Ball. No runs, one hit, no errors." A dreadful debut inning for Ruth, yet miraculously no runs scored. His inaugural bath over, Ruth allowed just five hits the rest of the way, shutting out the Bisons for a 6-0 win. There were, however, only about 200 fans there to see it. By the end of the first week of May, the Orioles were in second place, but the Terrapins were in first. The local papers didn't even bother to send a writer along with Dunn's team on their first road trip.

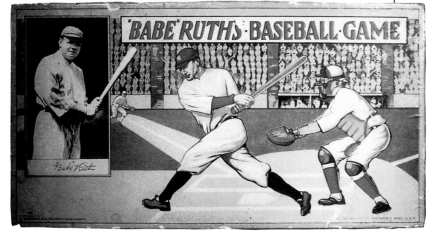

That road trip was a new step in Babe Ruth's education. For the first time, he visited large, bustling cities, sampling their wares (and wiles). Buffalo, Toronto, Montreal, Rochester, Boston, and

While the Babe rewrote the game on the field, he'd eventually have one in a box, too.

Honus Wagner, another outstanding ballplayer, resisted any temptation to jump ship to join the Federal League.

New York City (where the team stayed when they played Newark) opened their arms to the brash young star. He was having fun in a way he could never before have imagined.

By the end of May, Ruth was pitching well, although not consistently so. Fearful that his young prospect would be stolen by the Baltfeds—even though Hanlon had sworn he wouldn't raid his old friend's team and never did sign an Oriole player—Dunn doubled Ruth's salary to $200 a month. This brought him to $1,200 for the year.

Years later Ruth "recalled" that in April of 1914 the Federal League had offered him a $10,000 signing bonus and a $10,000 salary, which he refused because he feared that American League president Ban Johnson would prove true to his vow to ban for life anyone who signed with the upstarts. Ruth's recollection is specious. While the Feds were throwing their money around to sign players, $20,000 for a 19-year-old who had never played a big league game (despite his potential) seems outrageous. By comparison, the Federal League offered Honus Wagner, already an all-time great, just $15,000 to play and manage.

By the end of June, Ruth had put together an 11-7 record in 21 games. Dunn then boosted his salary again, to $1,800 a year. Ruth must have thought himself a millionaire. Truth be told, Dunn's largesse was only in self-defense; he was losing money. Lots of it. When Ruth pitched five innings to beat Toronto 13-8 on June 25, the Terrapins played across the street to a large crowd. Only 20 people paid to see Ruth and the Orioles that day.

By early July, Dunn had met with a group of Richmond businessmen interested in purchasing a share of the Orioles and moving the team to their city. Dunn didn't want to leave. On July 8, he sold outfielder Birdie Cree to the Yankees for a figure announced as $8,000; the next day Deek Derrick and George Twombly were shipped to Cincinnati for a total of $15,000. Two stories in the *Baltimore Sun* on consecutive days hinted at what was to come. The headline on July 9 stated flatly, "All Orioles for Sale." The next day a brief biography of Ruth appeared, titled "The Rise of Babe Ruth: Playing Hookey from School Starts Him on Brilliant Career." In the story, Dunn compared Ruth to Walter Johnson, a bit of braggadocio that sounds a lot like a salesman trying to negotiate a better price for his product.

That same afternoon Dunn announced he had sold Babe Ruth, star pitcher Ernie Shore, and longtime catcher/coach Ben Egan to Boston. The price Red Sox owner Joseph Lannin paid for the three has been variously cited from $8,500 to $25,000.

Dunn had previously offered Ruth to Connie Mack, but Mack was also feeling the Federal League pinch and was just one year away from his first famous "fire sale," at which he sold off nearly an entire team of stars. Dunn failed to offer Ruth to McGraw. Not surprisingly, McGraw—also known as "Little Napoleon"—was infuriated, and his unforgiving rage may have cost him. A decade later, Dunn asked if McGraw wanted Lefty Grove and was snubbed. Dunn sold Grove for the remarkable sum of $100,600—to Connie Mack. Grove proceeded to build a career as one of the greatest lefthanded pitchers in history.

The Babe's career, meanwhile, was on track. Just four months and one week after he left Baltimore in a thunderous snowstorm on the first train ride of his life, Ruth was on his way to where he belonged— the big leagues.

Connie Mack (pictured here with player Ira Thomas) managed the Philadelphia A's for 50 years. He crafted—and destroyed—two dynasties during this time. Had Mack been in the financial position to purchase Ruth when Dunn offered him, the Babe's future may have turned out much differently. Just one year after Dunn made his offer, Mack had to sell off all his stars to keep afloat.

"The more I see of Babe, the more he seems a figure out of mythology."

—Burt Whitman, Boston sportswriter, 1918

JOURNEY TO BOSTON: THE ROOKIE COMES OF AGE

Previous page: *Babe Ruth* (second from right) *with several of his mates from the 1915 Boston Red Sox.*

Although he was brought along as a pitcher in the big leagues, his penchant for the long ball would not be kept hidden for long.

He came into town poor and alone; uncultured, untraveled, and uninhibited. He left less than six years later a young man of considerable wealth and fame, married with a large country home and more friends and creature comforts than he had ever imagined possible. His years in Boston marked a coming of age for George Ruth, a time when he not only conquered baseball but learned to enjoy the varied pleasures that his excellence and its financial rewards opened to him. After an upbringing of hardened discipline and little love, he burst forth at his newfound freedom with a healthy enthusiasm. Along the way, he became one of the greatest stars in American sports.

Ruth always seemed to be a man in motion, so it should come as no surprise that five hours after arriving in Boston's Back Bay Station at 10 A.M. on July 11, 1914, he was making his major-league pitching debut against the Cleveland Indians at Fenway Park. Allowing two singles in the first inning, he recovered to help nail one runner at home plate and pick Shoeless Joe Jackson off first to end the frame. Four months out of St. Mary's and he was already showing the poise of a major leaguer.

Relying mostly on speed and guile, Ruth took a 3-1 lead into the seventh. He was scheduled to bat in the bottom of the inning, but then the Indians rallied with three singles to tie the contest. In his first two at bats against left-hander Willie Wilson, Babe had struck out and flied to right. When his time came again, Boston manager Bill Carrigan sent up veteran Duffy Lewis to pinch-hit. Lewis promptly scratched out an infield single and came around to score. When the lead held up,

George Ruth had won his first major-league game.

Although the tactic worked, it is difficult today—with the luxury of hindsight—to imagine anyone intentionally taking the bat out of the Babe's hands. At the time, however, Carrigan's move made sense. Despite the bursts of power he had shown in Baltimore, Ruth was still a rookie who had hit .200 in the minors and was facing a fellow left-hander. Besides, pitchers were not expected to perform well at the plate. The brash youngster would fight for more time in the batting cage during ensuing weeks, but Ruth's status became clear when he discovered one day that teammates had sawed the handles off his bats. He was there to *pitch*, not hit, and even this arrangement looked to be short-lived. Knocked out of the box by the Tigers early in his second start, Babe was relegated to the benchfor a month—where he watched former Orioles teammate Ernie Shore meet instant success on the mound.

Ernie Shore, once an Oriole teammate of Ruth's, was a pitcher for the Red Sox, too.

The Red Sox were not an easy ballclub to break into at the time. They had christened brand new Fenway Park with a world championship in 1912, and much of the nucleus of that team was still intact. Leading the group was Carrigan, a no-nonsense manager who also served as the team's catcher and had earned the nickname "Rough" for his playing style and discipline toward players. The outfield of Tris Speaker, Harry Hooper, and Lewis was among baseball's best; Speaker was also generally recognized as one of the game's greatest hitters. Larry Gardner was a solid third baseman and fine batsman, and the durable Ev-

The young, talented Boston hurler took advantage of the opportunity to learn from the more experienced players on his team.

With a deep pitching staff in Boston, the Babe found himself shipped down to the Providence Grays. He would not, however, make the trip alone.

Helen Woodford was only 16 when she met Babe at the restaurant where she worked as a waitress. He may have paid for his coffee, but he stole her heart.

erett Scott had taken over at short—where he would remain for 1,307 consecutive games.

The pitching staff was a deep combination of veterans and new-comers. Joe Wood and Ray Collins were the mainstays, and youngsters Shore (10-4), Dutch Leonard (19-5), and Rube Foster (14-8) were all turning in great seasons. Even during an off year when Boston finished second, it was easy to see why Ruth was expendable. In August of that season, he was demoted to the Providence Grays—an International League rival of Baltimore and another club just purchased by Boston owner Joe Lannin.

His teammates did not shed many tears at his departure. Despite the fanfare that had surrounded the arrival of Lannin's "$10,000 baby," Ruth was widely disliked for his crude manner, wild eating habits, and a carefree playing style that hard-nosed veterans viewed as lackadaisical. These same qualities would soon endear Babe to millions, but they were unacceptable coming from an unproven rookie. Once during warmups, a ball got away from Wood and rolled toward Ruth who, despite Wood's calls for assistance, intentionally let it pass between his legs with an exaggerated spread-eagle stance. Wood exploded, Ruth shouted back, and Carrigan had to restore order. Babe was troubled by such incidents but was able to seek refuge in the time he spent with a quiet, pretty 16-year-old waitress. He had met Helen Woodford while stopping into a coffee shop his first day in town, and the pair were dating regularly when he got the order to report 40 miles south to Providence.

Ruth's August 20 debut for the second-place Grays included the type of drama he would soon be enjoying on a regular basis. Pitching before an overflow crowd of 12,000—then the largest ever to see a baseball game in Rhode Island—he earned a 5-4 victory and helped his own cause by tripling twice. The performance was the springboard to a pennant for Providence, with Ruth going 9-2 in less than a month's work. Recalled to the Red Sox for the final week of the season, he drew a start from Carrigan and gained his first of many victories (along with his first major-league hit, a single) against the hapless New York Yankees. Nobody in Boston really noticed; up the street from Fenway, the "Miracle" Braves were completing a last-to-first climb up the standings that would culminate in a World Series sweep of Connie Mack's mighty Philadelphia Athletics.

There had been rough spots, but all told it had not been a bad year for George Ruth. Leaving the gates of St. Mary's in May a poor, foul-mannered kid, he returned to Baltimore six months later a local celebrity after going 23-8 at the highest level of minor league baseball and 2-1 in the big leagues. He had fallen in love (he and Helen married in October), earned more money then he'd ever seen—going from a $600 salary to $3,500 in one season—and spent it as fast as it came in. He had gotten his first driving license, had his first car accident, and experienced the pleasures of life on the road and in the big cities of the East Coast. Perhaps just as important at this point in his life's journey, Babe had realized there was more to life than shirtmaking and playing ball. He now seemed intent on finding out just how much of this new world he could make his own.

Young Babe and an even-younger Helen began their life together, and all seemed right with the world. He was earning more money than he ever had before and doing what he loved—playing baseball.

This picture of the youthful couple, presented to Helen's parents shortly after they were married, captures a more serious mood.

During the winter of 1914, Babe and Helen stayed in the apartment above his father's bar. The resemblance between father and son is extraordinary. George Sr. is pictured at far right; George Jr. is behind the punch bowl.

For the winter of 1914, he and Helen honeymooned in the flat they shared above the saloon where Babe tended bar with his father. When Ruth reported to spring training in 1915, he was a 21-year-old man, legally freed from the Brothers of St. Mary's and ready to crack Boston's deep starting rotation. The prospects didn't look good at first, but when rookie righthander Carl Mays went down with an April ankle injury, Babe got the call. After being hammered early in his first start, he lost his second outing 4-3 to the Yankees in a 13-inning contest. Carrigan was nonetheless impressed with Ruth's aggressiveness and a little something extra—a home run into the upper right field stands of the Polo Grounds. The 5,000-some onlookers that day were amazed at both its majesty and the ease with which it had been struck. This marked George Ruth's first homer in the major leagues.

Red Sox (and Yankee) fans would be getting plenty more of those in the future, but for now pitching was Ruth's main responsibility. Following a 1-4 start, he soon became one of the best in the business. Babe went 17-4 the rest of the way as Boston roared back from a shaky first month to win the AL pennant. His best pitch remained the fastball, but he had developed a strong curve as well. By watching and talking to veteran hurlers, he was able to improve his control as the season progressed. However rambunctious he got off the field, Ruth was proving a keen student of the game.

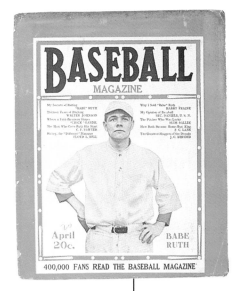

400,000 FANS READ THE BASEBALL MAGAZINE

Ruth was making a name for himself on the field. His style of play was refreshing, and the fans ate it up. Soon, he began to grace the covers of sporting journals, spreading his fast-growing fame even farther.

Between games, it was another story. Ruth had a voracious appetite for all life had to offer. Perhaps he was trying to make up for lost time. One could argue that, after living in virtual poverty, he was simply compensating. It soon became evident, though, that this would not be a passing phase. The frequency and flamboyancy of his escapades set him apart from other ballplayers. This became a common theme in the life Ruth was forming for himself—whatever he did, he did with gusto. He drove fast and recklessly, wore flashy, garish suits, and tales of his eating a dozen hot dogs and bottles of pop in a sitting (even indulging on the bench during games) were becoming legend. It was as if he was not sure his good fortune would last. Ruth seemed to be attempting to make up for two decades of neglect as quickly as he could.

As he proved himself on the field, teammates (most of whom weren't choirboys themselves) began accepting Ruth's zest for life and boisterous, sometimes vulgar banter around the clubhouse. Like Dunn in Baltimore, Manager Carrigan tried to curtail Babe's spending sprees by banking his salary (guaranteed for three years) and giving it to him in tiny daily installments—but the method seldom worked. Ruth respected the no-nonsense Carrigan as he would no other manager, but his fondness for good times went beyond his loyalties to any man, except perhaps Brother Matthias.

There was little time for Carrigan to worry about his wild young star, however; the Sox were in the middle of a furious pennant race with the Detroit Tigers that would go down to the wire. Taking first place in July, Boston at one point won 15 of 18 but barely gained ground on Detroit. A late-September series between the clubs at Fenway was expected to decide things, and the Red Sox won three of four—

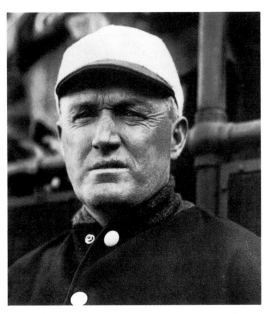

Bill Carrigan, manager of the Boston Red Sox. Although Carrigan achieved limited success in helping the Babe stick to training rules off the field, he couldn't argue with the results on the field.

Ruth claiming a 3-2 victory in the all-important final game. Boston wrapped the pennant up shortly thereafter.

The finish overshadowed another aspect of Babe's play that had been gaining momentum and attention that summer: his power. Ruth was evolving into an individual who radiated a magnetic exuberance, and his proficiency in hitting balls long distances fit right in with his character. It was an act fans had not seen in some time; the home run had not been a significant part of the game in decades. In fact, the league leaders in this category rarely had more than a dozen. Baseball was in its so-called dead-ball era, when batting averages hovered around .250 and steals, hit-and-run plays, and bunts were the preferred offense. The baseballs used in the games were scuffed, dirtied, and greased up by pitchers (the spitball was not outlawed until 1921) and were often left in games long after they had grown threadbare or water-logged.

Perennial batting champ Ty Cobb—a .367 lifetime hitter who stole as many as 96 bases in a season—was the game's greatest star during this period despite never hitting more than nine home runs before 1921. Cobb's maniacal mastery of the base-by-base, low-scoring "inside" baseball included spike-first slides, but with a $20,000 contract, he had plenty of men trying to emulate it. There seemed no real reason to believe the game was due for change, but eventually—albeit gradually at first—Ruth would change it.

No statistics for home runs were recorded in newspapers during 1915, but if there had been, Red Sox fans would have seen Ruth's name atop their team list with four (the rest of the club altogether had totaled just 10). Babe's flowing, upward stroke was a rare sight in a league of level swingers hoping just to make solid contact. When he connected, the ball was apt to go far. He hit only the second homer to ever reach the distant right field bleachers of Fenway Park, and his final shot of the year in St. Louis completely left Sportsman's Park before bouncing across a street and reportedly breaking the plate-glass window of an automobile dealership 430 feet from home plate.

Teammate Joe Dugan said that Babe "swung from Port Arthur, Texas, on every pitch." One of the reasons for such force was the sheer brawn of the man supplying it. The average major leaguer of the time stood around 5'9" and weighed under 170 pounds; at 6'2" and 190 pounds, Ruth had a dramatic, imposing presence on the field. He had huge shoulders and arms, a firm chest, and tiny, splintery legs that made him appear almost cartoonish while running.

This team photograph of the 1915 Red Sox shows Ruth (third row, standing fifth from right) in his rookie season. Carl Mays, who would later become better known for one fateful pitch rather than the rest of his career, is standing to the right of Babe.

He could run, however, and run well; the massive belly and slow gait that modern fans have come to accept as a standard part of his physique would come much later. Indeed, 1915 saw Ruth as a lean, muscular man, whose body had been hardened by the tough and disciplined life of St. Mary's. He wasn't fatter than everyone else then, just bigger.

His facial features were also distinctive. Ruth's face was defined by small, squinting eyes, a broad, flat nose, and large lips. Reporters and fans everywhere were just beginning to discover the uni-

Babe Ruth: His Life and Times

The arms that carried the BoSox. From left, Shore, Wood, Foster, and Ruth. These hurlers comprised one of the AL's best staffs.

versal appeal of this gregarious, funny-looking youngster, and Ruth was basking in the attention.

For now, however, he was but one star on a pennant-winning team that had recorded an impressive 101-50 regular season record. He had hit .315, and with 10 doubles and a triple to go with his four homers in just 92 at bats, he had a tidy .576 slugging average. This mark was some .250 above the league average. The numbers matched nicely alongside his 18-8 record and 2.44 ERA as a pitcher, but despite a handful of pinch-hitting appearances (he went 1 for 10), Babe was still counted on mostly for his hurling. The hits were a helpful bonus; the Red Sox had only outfielders Speaker (.322) and Lewis (.291) regularly contributing to a shaky offense, but Ruth, Foster (19-8), Shore (18-8), Leonard (15-7), and Wood (15-5) comprised the American League's deepest starting staff. If any of them got in trouble, Mays now waited in the bullpen.

While the Babe was a member of the world-champion Sox, his bat had really yet to be heard from. He wasn't doing too poorly on the mound, however. The Bambino managed a 2.44 ERA in 1915.

The youngster among this sextet, Ruth pitched nine innings in a meaningless doubleheader at season's end while the others were rested in anticipation of the upcoming World Series against the Philadelphia Phillies. This indicated Babe wouldn't get a Series start, and that was indeed the case. He did see action as a pinch-hitter in the ninth inning of the third game (Carrigan now showing considerable confidence in his batting) but bounced out to first with a man on base in a 2-1 loss. He was frustrated by the experience, but his mood was likely tempered somewhat when the Red Sox went on to win the Series in five games. This feat earned Ruth a $3,780.25 winner's share—nearly $300 more than his annual salary.

Ruth had joined the Red Sox at a very opportune time financially. The establishment of another major league during 1914 and 1915—the Federal League—had forced American and National League owners to pay higher salaries to keep their players from jumping ship. The practice held true especially for the bigger stars of the game, but it trickled down through the ranks all the way to rookies. Although several players did make the leap, the ownership strategy eventually did the trick; the Federal League did not survive into the 1916 season, and owners were able to go back to their parsimonious ways.

This inevitably led to salary disputes in 1915 as stars fought to avoid pay cuts. The Red Sox had two of the most celebrated players of the time: Speaker refused to sign through spring training when Lannin announced he was cutting him from $15,000 to $9,000, and the frail-armed Wood failed to report altogether when his salary was slashed even more

dramatically. Boston players continued to remain optimistic that their stars would soon be under wraps; after all, the Red Sox were a championship team. Even when Lannin purchased the outfielder Clarence "Tilly" Walker from Connie Mack's A's, the transaction was looked at as solely an insurance move,

This interesting moment was captured at Red Sox training camp in 1916. In retrospect, it gives one an entertaining way to credit Ruth with having a hand in ending the dead-ball era.

what with Lewis hurting and spring training less than a week away.

A few days later, however, Speaker was sold to the Cleveland Indians for $50,000 and two unknowns (one of whom turned out to be Sad Sam Jones, a fine pitcher). It was the most shocking and disarming news Boston baseball fans had ever heard, not to be surpassed until another outfielder was banished from Boston a few

Smokey Joe Wood, the right-handed hurler from Kansas City, had his best season with the 1912 Boston Red Sox. That year he topped the league in wins (34), winning percentage (.872), complete games (35), and shutouts (10).

years later—but that's another story. Speaker brought in the largest amount ever paid for a player, but no one except Lannin cared about the money when the cost was a .344 lifetime hitter and the leader of the World Series champs. It was also effectively the end of Wood's Boston career; he never did sign with the Red Sox, instead joining his friend and roommate in Cleveland the next spring.

The move threatened to spoil the cohesiveness of the club, but winning has a way of solving all problems. Taking the ball on Opening Day in 1916, Ruth won 2-1 to start the Sox off to a streak of six victories in their first eight games. His second appearance was a matchup with Washington Senators right-hander Walter Johnson, considered by most the best and fastest pitcher in the game. Ruth emerged victorious again in a 5-1 decision. It was his second triumph over Johnson in as many meetings, and Babe would eventually rack up six consecutive victories against The Big Train (five of the wins would be marked by just a one-run difference) while establishing himself as one of baseball's dominant hurlers.

Ruth won his first four starts to help the Red Sox into first place, but, hurt by the loss of Speaker, the club suddenly dropped into a horrendous batting slump. Even in the dry offensive spell, however, Ruth usually pitched—and hit—well enough to win. He out-dueled Johnson again in a 1-0 victory on June 1, then tossed another shutout four days later against Cleveland. He lost his next start against Detroit but was perfect at the plate and hit his first home run since the previous July. He homered again (a three-run shot) when Carrigan called on him to pinch-hit three days later at St. Louis. Pitching the next afternoon's game, the Babe beat the Browns 5-3 while homering for the third time in as many games.

Now that Ruth's average was up over .300, nobody was about to saw his bats in half anymore. There was talk of moving Babe to a position where he could play every day, but Carrigan never really considered it. As weak as the Red Sox were offensively, the conservative manager felt pitching and defense would still be the keys to the club repeating as champions. Ruth, it appeared, was not only the best pitcher Carrigan now had on his staff but also the finest in the league. Perhaps to drive his point home even more, he kept Babe in the ninth spot in the batting order—the traditional spot for pitchers to be in the lineup.

The Red Sox remained in third place entering July but then caught fire. Ruth won four straight in one stretch, including another 1-0 win over Walter Johnson—this one a 13-inning affair—and Boston took a 6½-game lead. Another slump hit, and the Red Stockings had dropped back to third place entering their final western road swing. It was then that the Babe was called upon to save the season. Facing the second-place White Sox before a crowd of over 40,000—at that time the largest to gather in Chicago baseball history—Babe earned his 20th victory with a 6-2 win to move Boston back into second. (Drawing record-number crowds, by the way, was becoming a regular event for Babe.) A Shore victory the next day, coupled with a loss by the first-place Tigers, put Boston into the lead, and a three-game sweep of Detroit the following week essentially wrapped up the pennant.

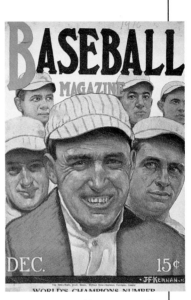

Carrigan and company would again grace the cover of Baseball Magazine *at the end of the 1916 season. It would be the last hurrah for the retiring manager.*

Ruth and teammate Dick Hoblitzel engage in a friendly bout of fisticuffs in 1916. The two were good friends off the field, and their families even vacationed together.

His success against Johnson and in the season's biggest games had earned Ruth status as the ace of Boston's pitching staff. At age 21, he was now arguably the best left-hander in baseball. Compiling a 23-13 record for the season, he ranked third in the American League in wins, innings ($323^{2}/_{3}$), and strikeouts (170) while setting a league record for left-handers with nine shutouts that still stands. Only Chicago's Eddie Cicotte bettered Babe's .657 winning percentage, and Ruth's league-best 1.75 ERA has not been topped by a Red Sox pitcher since. He held opponents to a .201 batting average (also the lowest mark in the league) and when at the plate himself batted .272 including 19 pinch-hitting appearances.

Boston faced the Brooklyn Robins in the World Series, and this time Ruth would play a major role. Shore won 6-5 in the opener at Braves Field, and Babe started Game 2 before a delighted crowd of 41,373 and threatening skies. Dark clouds

Repeat! Boston went the distance for the second season in a row in 1916. In addition to the loss of Speaker, there had been at least one other significant difference in this championship. This year, Ruth had been allowed to make a major contribution.

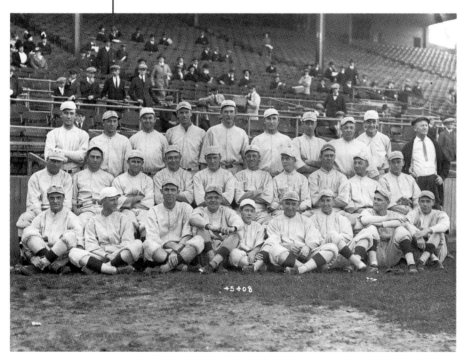

drifted in over the park as the game got underway. Conditions in the park looked ominous for Boston when the third man up for Brooklyn smashed a line drive to center that bounced to the wall for an inside-the-park homer as outfielders Walker and Hooper stumbled in pursuit.

Trailing 1-0, Ruth escaped further trouble in the third when Robins pitcher Sherry Smith was tagged out trying to stretch a double into a triple. Babe got a reprieve with an RBI ground out later the same inning, and it would remain 1-1 for 11 more frames. Both teams had scoring chances thwarted by baserunning blunders. As the sky grew darker, Ruth seemed to get stronger. After allowing six hits and three walks through seven innings, he had relinquished just one

walk and no hits over the next seven. When Boston came to bat in the bottom of the 14th, the umpires declared this would be the last half-inning.

First baseman Dick Hoblitzel led off with a walk (his fourth of the game against Sherry) and was sacrificed to second by Lewis. Pinch-hitter Del Gainor followed with a line drive over the head of the third baseman (who probably had trouble seeing it in the dark), and the winning run scored in what was then the longest World Series game ever played. Joe Lannin probably had mixed emotions about the whole thing. Had the game remained tied through 14 innings, the umpires had ruled the contest would have been started from scratch the following day—a move which would have most likely netted the host Red Sox some $100,000 in additional revenue.

Ruth's excitement over his first Series win was evident as he leaped about the clubhouse. "I told you a year ago I could take care of those National League bums, and you never gave me the chance," he yelled at Carrigan. The manager's warm reply of "Forget about it, Babe," possibly stemmed from the fact that Carrigan knew he would no longer have to put up with Ruth's shenanigans following the season. The manager had announced his retirement (to be effective at season's end) during September. After the Red Sox dispatched of the Phillies in five games for their second straight world championship, the old catcher waved goodbye to a record 42,620 fans at Braves Field and headed for his home in Maine to stay.

A meet and greet session for the champions. Students at a Plymouth, New Hampshire, school were delighted to have the opportunity to say hello and get a handshake from the Boston stars. Note how the Babe stands out in a crowd.

Babe and fellow pitcher Herb Pennock. In 1916, Pennock started off with Boston but was sent to Buffalo for more seasoning. They would team up again, but in different uniforms.

For Ruth and his teammates, however, it was off to New Hampshire for a post-season hunting trip with their wives. Another winner's share—$3,780.25, more than his yearly salary—pushed Babe's earnings for the season up to nearly $7,500. This was in an era when new cars could be had for a few hundred bucks. He had no problem spending the loot quickly. The purchase of an 80-acre spread in suburban Sudbury, Massachusetts, (20 miles from Boston) gave Babe and Helen their first real home, and the place was fittingly named "Home Plate Farm." Although Helen would spend much time there over the next several years, her husband found it too quiet to frequent on a regular basis. There was too much fun to be had out in the world, and right now the fun looked like it would never end.

Bill Carrigan was not the only prominent member of Boston's World Series winners who would not be around the following spring. Suffering from a bad heart, upset over Carrigan's retirement, and troubled with the fan backlash from the Speaker deal, Joe Lannin announced on November 1 that he was selling the club for $650,000 to a trio of investors. The leading shareholder and most prominent among the group was New York theatrical producer Harry Frazee—a man who would later become known as the greatest villain in the history of the Red Sox.

Frazee was a self-made entertainment czar. Having risen from life as a bellhop in Peoria, Illinois, to owner of two of the nation's leading theaters, Frazee would prove a shrewd charmer who convinced Boston fans he had their best interests at heart. Truth be told, his mind and heart were usually looking ahead to his next show. After

Helen and Babe became fond of spending time in the outdoors. For Babe, however, the draw of city life and all its trappings held greater appeal.

The Babe could not have imagined all the changes that were in store after manager Bill Carrigan retired and Joe Lannin sold the ball club.

taking over one of baseball's leading teams, he would take less than five years to decimate it and shift the American League's base of power from Boston to New York. While the Yankees would go on to championship after championship, the Red Sox would be floundering near or at the bottom of the AL for over a decade.

None of this could be imagined early on. Frazee spent his first months as president trying to convince Carrigan to return as manager, while also supposedly negotiating a $60,000 deal for Walter Johnson. Both attempts failed (the latter was later suspected as a public relations scam), but fans appreciated the effort. Frazee even claimed he was willing to take all necessary steps to become a Massachusetts resident, as long as he could return to New York each New Year's Eve. "Harry Frazee, at least, combines experience in the game [with] a genuine love for it," stated the *Boston Globe*. "Like Joe Lannin, he is a fan 'from way back,' and that is reassuring to the fans of Boston and New England."

George Ruth was undoubtedly among Frazee's admirers. Heeding a warning from AL President Ban Johnson that "extravagances, especially salaries, must be reduced" for the league to remain profitable, Frazee had cut several salaries and offered just few raises to his World Series winners. One of the raises, however, went

While the threat of war loomed heavy on the horizon, baseball seemed to hang in the balance. AL President Ban Johnson encouraged the teams to run drills and to be prepared to do their part if the call should come.

to Ruth, whose annual pay jumped from $3,500 to $5,000. Pleased, Babe reported to spring training at Hot Springs, Arkansas, fit in mind and body and with Helen in tow.

His happiness reached new heights as he found himself more easily accepted as a veteran star by his teammates. It was a loose, carefree camp under Frazee's new manager (and second baseman) Jack Barry, and Ruth's loud laugh was a welcome sound in the bowling alleys and at poker games. The atmosphere in the real world was growing tense with the increased threat of America entering into World War I, but even an order from Ban Johnson for teams to begin instituting drill practice was quickly ignored. Only when President Woodrow Wilson officially declared war on Germany on April 2 did the Red Sox and other clubs finally take heed—and ballplayers could be seen on the field and marching in time prior to the action on Opening Day.

"Babe" Ruth C.F. Yankees

There can be a high price to success. Babe, like many athletes once they have reached greatness, felt considerable pressure to excel.

Against this patriotic backdrop, Babe shut out the Yankees 10-0 in Boston's opener at the Polo Grounds. Ruth's newfound confidence was apparent immediately. He began arguing vehemently over balls and strikes with veteran umpire Tommy Connolly. When he was called out on strikes himself in the seventh inning, he turned dramatically and glared at Connolly before retreating to the bench. It was the type of behavior that has sometimes come back to haunt pitchers, but despite his outbursts, Ruth won his first eight decisions, and the Red Sox moved into first place with a 15-5 start.

Exempted from the draft because of his marital status, Ruth could relax when other major leaguers marched off to register in early June. Still, the pressure to retain his place atop the league's pitching charts seemed to be getting to him. He showed tremendous frustration following a 3-0 loss to Cleveland in which he had the only Red Sox hit and allowed his discouragement to carry over onto the field of play. On June 23, the Red Sox were facing the Washington Senators.

A bit of foreshadowing? The Bambino warms up before a game against the Yankees in April 1917.

After getting behind in the count to the leadoff man, words were exchanged between Ruth and home plate umpire Clarence "Brick" Owens. The tension between the hurler and the official continued to mount with each pitch. Finally, Ruth made a trip to the plate for a little discussion with the ump.

When Owens warned him to go back to the mound or face dismissal, Ruth replied to Owens that he would "bust you one on the nose" if he was run out. Owens proceeded to run him out. Finally, in total frustration, the Babe snapped and charged at the ump, landing a fat punch on his nose. Needless to say, this outburst caused him to be dismissed from the game.

Ed Barrow (Boston's manager of choice for 1918) and Red Sox owner Harry Frazee sit down to discuss contractual agreements with players Ruth and Stuffy McInnis. Frazee's fondness for show tunes ended up costing him more than money.

Barry motioned for Shore to come in and relieve, and after the legal limit of eight warm-up tosses, Eddie delivered his first pitch to the second batter. Just then Morgan broke from first in a surprise steal attempt and was nabbed at second on a throw from Thomas. Shore proceeded to set down the next 26 batters in order, and since all 27 outs of the contest were retired with him on the mound, he received credit for a perfect game—just the fourth in major league history—in Boston's 4-0 win. Of the fisticuffs with the official, Babe would later remark, "It wasn't a love tap. I really socked him—right in the jaw."

Babe was suspended indefinitely by Ban Johnson for the scuffle. It was only after some smooth talking by Frazee that he was reinstated after 10 days with only a $100 fine. Whether the incident shook up the club or not, it marked the beginning of a slide for the Red Sox that saw them drop behind surging Chicago in the American League. The rest of the season saw the Red Sox take first only briefly (in July). Boston eventually finished in second place, nine games back. It would mark the only time in the four years from 1915 through 1918 that they would not be the winners of the World Series.

As for the Babe, he recovered from his slip-up to turn in his second consecutive outstanding season—and his most durable. Going 24-13 to finish second in the AL in wins, he also placed third in the circuit with 326⅓ innings, finished fifth with 128 strikeouts, and led the majors with an incredible 35 complete games in 38 starts. He also ranked high with a 2.01 ERA and six shutouts. While Barry seemed even less willing to let him pinch hit than Carrigan, Ruth still batted .325 with two homers. One of these long-distance shots included the first ever struck into the deepest center field bleachers at Fenway.

Babe was discovering that his talents could reap big rewards.

The lack of a championship was disappointing, but Ruth had settled into a comfortable position in Boston. He and Frazee seemed to get along fine, the slick showman apparently taking to the brash young hurler with his own flair for the dramatic. When Ruth got into trouble again shortly following the season, the owner let it go without comment. Involved in an automobile accident, the Babe escaped injury, and the unfortunate occurrence didn't garner much bad press. While Frazee probably was not too thrilled, 24-game winners who could hit .325 were hard to come by.

The war caused even more changes in the Red Sox makeup before the start of the 1918 season. Single men who had signed up for the reserves the previous summer were called up for active duty, and this included Lewis, Shore, and player-manager Jack Barry. Again Frazee was in the market for a manager, and this time he wanted someone willing to help with the day-to-day executive duties of running the ballclub as well. The answer was Ed Barrow, who was in the midst of being forced into resigning from his position as president of the floundering International League. A tough and confident man, Barrow had managed, promoted, and owned clubs at various professional levels but had less than two years major league managerial experience. Suddenly both a field and general manager, he would prove quite competent at handling both posts.

Finding ways to replace nearly a dozen players gone or expected to go into the service was Frazee's other main concern. Unlike more conservative owners who chose to wait the war out with whatever talent remained on their rosters, "Big Harry" took out his checkbook and went about improving his club. Philadelphia Athletics owner Connie Mack was selling off the last of the remaining regulars from his great championship teams of 1910 to '14. For $60,000 and three second-liners, Frazee was able to pick up pitcher Joe Bush, catcher Wally Schang, and outfielder Amos Strunk. Another deal with Mack a month later—Frazee gave up Larry Gardner and two lesser players this time—brought in first baseman Stuffy McInnis.

Ruth wanted in on Frazee's spending spree and asked for a 100 percent raise to $10,000 a year. Frazee balked, joking that "I've never paid an actor that much." Eventually, they agreed to a deal in which Frazee gave Ruth $7,000 for 1918 and promised him $10,000 for the following season were he to turn in a good year. Just what constituted a good year wasn't exactly known, but Babe intended to leave no

Under the expert leadership of Ed Barrow, the 1918 Boston Red Sox were in for a spectacular season. Babe (back row, fourth from left), the Opening Day starter for the third year running, came away with another victory.

doubt he deserved the five figures. Performing well in spring training despite having ballooned in the off-season to over 215 pounds, Ruth played first base in two exhibition games and hit three homers—including a grand slam. Then it was back to the mound.

Babe was the Opening Day starter for the third straight year and for the third time came away with a victory. The quartet of Ruth, Mays, Leonard, and Bush was the steadiest in baseball (none ever missing his spot in the rotation) over the season's first month, but once again the Red Sox were not hitting much. When Ruth slugged his first homer of the season over the roof of the Polo Grounds on May 4 (against, who else, the Yankees), it brought to light the same old question: Why not try and get his bat in the lineup every day?

Apparently Harry Hooper had been discussing this very topic with Barrow on a regular basis. With service duties and injuries plaguing his regular lineup, the manager finally relented by letting Babe play first base and bat sixth against the Yankees

On the threshold of greatness. In 1918, Ruth tied for the lead in home runs (11) with Clarence "Tilly" Walker of Philadelphia. Although the Babe would top many categories for more than a decade to come, those in baseball were about to discover that the advent of the home run as a legitimate weapon was upon them.

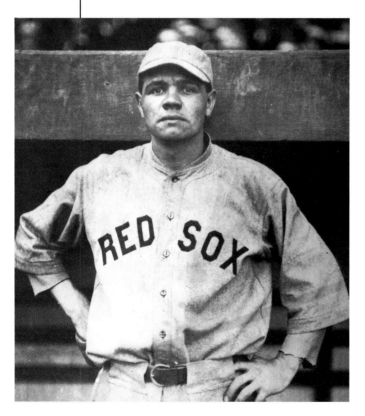

on May 6. Three years to the day after hitting his first major-league home run in the same ballpark, Ruth homered again at the Polo Grounds before a crowd that included both Frazee and Yankees owner Jacob Ruppert. No doubt realizing that this was the fifth of Ruth's 11 career homers hit in his yard, Ruppert supposedly offered to buy the young slugger on the spot. Frazee declined, but it was an omen.

The next day in Washington, Ruth was at first base again and homered for the third straight game—the second time he had accomplished this rare feat. He doubled while playing first base the next day, then returned to the mound the following afternoon and worked 10 innings in a 4-3 loss—notching a

single, three doubles, and a triple in the process. Babe was suddenly hitting .484 and was the talk of baseball. Conversely, the Red Sox were on a six-game losing streak. Barrow may have had thoughts of ending the experiment then, but Boston was returning home, and he knew Babe's presence would draw huge crowds. After all, Barrow had a $50,000 investment in the club.

Ruth was in a new position—left field—the next day at Fenway Park, and perhaps unnerved by the switch, he went hitless to break a 10-game batting streak. Back at first base the following afternoon, he had three hits, fielded well, and drew raucous applause each time he approached the plate. Ruth's hitting fell off as he battled a sore throat, and when the sickness worsened he was scratched from a scheduled pitching start May 20 and sent home. The team trainer accompanied him, and along the way they stopped into a drugstore where the trainer treated Babe's throat by swabbing it with silver nitrate (then a common prescription). The pain and choking that ensued landed Ruth in the hospital, where his condition was diagnosed as swelling of the larynx and labeled serious.

Ruth remained in the hospital a week and later would attribute his trademark husky voice to the incident. He was back with the club on May 30 but received just one pinch-hitting appearance before pitching three days later. He lost the game despite hitting a home run, then was moved back to the outfield where he homered each of the next three days. Babe was starting to really enjoy himself, and when his turn to pitch came around again he told Barrow he was no longer interested. He wanted to be out there hitting every day.

Barrow agreed at first. Sad Sam Jones was able to step in and pitch well in Ruth's absence, but when Dutch Leonard jumped the club to take a shipyard job and avoid being drafted, the manager wanted Ruth back in the rotation. Ruth, claiming a wrist injury, refused. After a brief benching, Babe returned to the regular lineup and hit three homers in little over a week. He now had 11 home runs on the season—a figure reached by just three American Leaguers in the previous 15 years—and it was only June 30.

Despite turmoil in his personal life, Ruth's feats on the field were popular with the fans.

An argument caused Barrow to fine Ruth $500. The Babe, distressed by the situation, stormed from the clubhouse and retreated to his father's home. Meanwhile, the team traveled on to Philadelphia, and two days later headlines blared that Ruth was quitting the Red Sox to play for a Pennsylvania shipyard team. Eventually things were ironed out and Ruth returned, ostensibly to play the outfield and pitch when needed.

Baseball received a scare when its new classification as a job nonessential to the war effort suddenly left hundreds of players open to the draft, but a compromise was made in which all players were allowed to stay on provided the season end a month early on Labor Day. His compromise with Barrow had Ruth pitching every fourth day down the stretch. When Ruth won seven games in little over a month, he helped the Red Sox to their third pennant in four years. He wound up 13-7 overall with a 2.22 ERA and 18 complete games in 19 starts. Despite this illustrious feat, it was in 59 outfield games and 13 at first base that Ruth had provided the most excitement.

His home run power mysteriously vanished the final two months, but despite just 317 at bats, Babe's 11 homers still tied him for the major league lead. His 66 RBI (tied for third) and 26 doubles (second) ranked high as well, and he was the only .300 hitter on the team. While he also set the standard with 59 strikeouts, this only added to his popularity. Fans loved watching him miss and wind up in his trademark pretzel-like position almost as much as they enjoyed seeing him connect.

Boston had a 21-game winner in Carl Mays, but Barrow fooled almost everyone by starting Ruth in the World Series opener against the Chicago Cubs on

September 5 at Wrigley Field. People had expected Babe to be in left field the first contest, but instead he tossed a six-hit 1-0 shutout and set up the winning run with a fourth-inning single off Hippo Vaughn. Once more Ruth was the center of attention.

The teams split the next two contests, and Ruth was slated to start Game Four in Boston. Babe hurt the middle knuckle of his pitching hand horsing around on the train home. Despite struggling throughout the contest, he managed to earn a 3-2 victory, thanks to relief help in the ninth and his own two-run triple. He also shut out the Cubs over the first seven innings, giving him 29 consecutive scoreless frames over three games (including one in the '16 Series) to break Christy Mathewson's record of 28 set in 1905. Ruth's mark would stand 42 years, and he would always label it his proudest accomplishment in baseball—greater than any of his batting feats.

The final two games were tainted by a thwarted player strike over record-low Series shares, but the Red Sox won nonetheless to claim their fifth World Championship overall without a loss. They were a strong team that expected to be on top for years, with the 23-year-old Ruth their prize player. When the war ended two months later, fans began looking forward to an uninterrupted season when they could see their beloved team claim another flag. Little did they know how long the wait would be.

The off-season regimen for Ruth changed following the 1918 campaign, for there was no longer a father to go home to and help at the bar. A fistfight outside his tavern had left the elder George dead. Babe was officially the

With Ed Barrow (far left) at the helm, the Red Sox set off for another World Series. The wily manager proved he still had a few tricks up his sleeve. During this year's Series, the Babe accomplished feats he counted among his greatest.

orphan he had in effect been for years. He grew restless on the farm, and his night-time spending sprees continued. This prompted a plea to Frazee for another raise, from $7,000 to $15,000, a figure exceeded only by the great Ty Cobb. Ruth punctuated his demand with the stipulation that it be a *two-year* deal.

Frazee said no; between poor war-time attendance and the cost of purchasing star players, Big Harry was in big debt. He proved his point by selling Ernie Shore, Dutch Leonard, and Duffy Lewis to the Yankees, but Babe threatened again to quit baseball. Frazee didn't buy the threat for a moment.

Only when March came and the holdout threatened to affect his spring training gate receipts did Frazee relent. Babe had offered an alternative demand of $10,000 over three years, and it was accepted. Ruth promptly went south, and in Boston's first exhibition game versus the Giants, he hit a home run longer than anyone present could ever remember seeing. Legend has it traveling 600 feet or more, and it was a sign of what was to come. Babe took Duffy's vacated starting spot in left field and homered in a 10-0 Opening Day trouncing over New York. After several rainouts, the Babe added a double, two triples, and five runs scored in a pair of victories at Washington.

Ruth's nightly escapades reached new heights in the capital city, however, and star or no star the tough-minded Barrow wanted Babe to know who was boss. Eliciting the help of a night porter at the team hotel, Barrow was awakened at 6 A.M. and

The 1919 Boston Red Sox. That year, the Babe led the league in runs, homers, RBI, and on-base and slugging percentage. He also tallied nine wins.

told that the Babe had just come in. Storming into Ruth's room, he found the slugger in bed with the sheets pulled up—cigar lit and fully dressed. "You're a fine citizen, Babe," he reportedly shouted. "I must say, you're a fine citizen."

Initially embarrassed, Ruth was fuming when he arrived at the ballpark the next day and challenged the 50-year-old Barrow to a fight. Ed didn't back down. While a sparring match was avoided, Babe wound up on the bench. Only after an apology

and a promise to write Barrow a "Dear Eddie" note each night telling the manager what time he arrived back in was he allowed to play. He recovered from a .180 batting average (with just two home runs) the first month and proceeded to start hitting homers at a steady pace. Despite an earlier promise from Barrow that he would not have to pitch, he did come in from left field to go 5-2 by June 20.

The trio of star players sold to the Yankees were missed, as was pitcher Carl Mays, who was sold for $40,000 following an unexplained midseason walkout. Red Sox fans, no longer having a championship to hope for, increasingly turned their full attention to Ruth. He did not disappoint. Tying his old mark of 11 homers by mid-July, he went on to break Ned Williamson's major-league record of 27 (set in 1884) with a titanic shot over the Polo Grounds roof late in September.

Ruth's home run the last weekend of the season in Washington gave him the unique distinction of being the first player to homer in every city in the league, and his final totals of 29 homers, 114 RBI, 103 runs, a .657 slugging percentage, and a .456 on-base percentage all led the majors. He also went 9-5 with a 2.97 ERA on the mound, but nobody really cared. Even though the Red Sox were a sixth-place team, fans took great delight in having the game's greatest slugger to watch every day right in their own back yard.

Nobody could imagine what was coming. Fans would still be able to watch Ruth on a regular basis in 1920, but a change of mailing address would be necessary.

The Babe, his bat, and Boston—something was about to change. Here's a hint, the Babe and his bat would not soon be parted.

The face of the future. Just as owner Harry Frazee ignored business on the field, he also floundered in his attempt to become the prince of Broadway. He failed to realize that right under his nose, the heir-apparent to baseball's stage was coming to power.

"They'll never build any monuments to Harry Frazee in Boston."

—Babe Ruth, on his sale from Boston by the Red Sox owner

THE BABE HITS BROADWAY: LET THE REVOLUTION BEGIN

Previous page: Primed for his life as an entrepreneur, the Babe hands out his namesake cigars

$\mathcal{D}$espite Babe Ruth's record-breaking heroics for the sixth-place Red Sox, 1919 was destined to go down as the darkest year in baseball history. The American League Champion Chicago White Sox were upset by the Cincinnati Reds in a World Series filled with questionable defensive play by the defeated. Whispers soon began circulating of a fix between a gambling syndicate and Chicago players. When there proved to be some validity to the talk and the eight conspiring players were put on trial the following summer, fans grew disillusioned. The very integrity of the game was threatened.

Baseball's first commissioner—Judge Kenesaw Mountain Landis—was somewhat helpful in restoring the public trust. In October 1920, he banished the eight accused players from baseball for life. It was through another player's feats, however, that fans were truly able to put aside the ill feelings brought on by the "Black Sox" scandal as it unfolded. Ruth's 1920 season was so astounding that it defied comparison; his team set attendance records, his name was splashed across the headlines daily, and he quickly became a hero to millions in the cities where he played. His childish enthusiasm for the game, and indeed for life itself, prompted his ascent to the top of America's popularity charts. Even as the nation entered a decade of unparalleled free-spirited prosperity, Bostonians found themselves in a less than envious position. They could only look on from afar

Judge Kenesaw Mountain Landis, baseball czar.

as the most beloved rabble-rouser of them all went about his work.

The Babe, no longer a member of the Red Sox, was now working his magic for the citizens of New York.

The change of scenery for the Babe has an interesting bit of history behind it. The drop to the second division notwithstanding, the 1919 season had been exciting for Boston fans due to one simple reason—George Herman Ruth. His home runs kept folks cheering long after Boston's stake in the pennant race was decided, and his final total of 29 homers over the course of just 130 games was such an astronomical figure that many people didn't know what to make of it. American League home run champions over the previous decade (including Ruth the previous season) had averaged just 10 in their title years. Nate Seybold held the former AL record with 16, and Gavvy Cravath's 24 with the Phillies in 1915 had been the previous high by a modern player. Snooping historians had dug up Ned Williamson's 27-homer spree for the Cubs in 1884—a fluke effort aided by six-ball walks, underhand pitching, and a 215-foot right field fence in Chicago's home park that season—but Ruth topped that as well.

It was a crowd-pleasing performance, but not everybody within baseball was impressed. At the time Ruth came along, home runs just weren't a regular occurrence for the game. Some folks, including Ty Cobb, argued that such slugging would make a mockery of the

The 1919 White Sox had all the components to be the world champions. Due to low pay from a tightwad owner, however, they were easy prey for those with illicit interests.

Looking regal in his pinstripes, the Babe was a welcome sight for Yankees fans.

Dead-ball era star Ty Cobb resisted the changes that the Babe was ushering into baseball.

game's strategic makeup were it allowed to continue. This seems absurd now; scoring as many as four runs with one swing seems like pretty good offensive strategy.

One must remember that swinging for the fences was a new style then and contrasted sharply with the base-to-base "inside" baseball Cobb and others thrived on. Only five major leaguers besides Ruth hit as many as 10 homers in 1919 (none more than Cravath's 12). While Babe's total topped that of 10 big league teams, including both pennant-winners, it was not enough to help Boston to even so much as a .500 record.

"Given the proper equipment, which consists solely in the strength to knock a ball forty feet farther than the average man can do it, anybody can play big league baseball today," a disgusted Cobb noted. "In other words, science is out the window."

Contrary to what Cobb and others thought of homers, Ruth's slugging had certainly not cost Boston the pennant. The Red Sox finished 66-71 because two of the best pitchers from their 1918 world championship club (Dutch Leonard and Carl Mays) had joined former Fenway favorites Duffy Lewis and Ernie Shore on the 1919 Yankees. Ruth's remaining teammates were a pretty sorry lot that produced a combined three home runs along with an aggregate 3.30 ERA—a mark exceeded by just two big league teams even when factoring in Babe's 2.97 mark. The only real bright spot amidst this gloom had been Ruth's longball exploits, and an overflow crowd of 31,000-

plus (including 5,000 roped off in the outfield) turned out at Fenway in late September to give him a "day." In an otherwise meaningless doubleheader, he tied Williamson's record and sent the packed house into a frenzy—nobody caring for the moment that the Sox were headed nowhere.

Harry Frazee could see the appeal his slugger had on fans, but even with a fine season turnout of 417,291 in attendance the owner wasn't making money quick enough. John Lannin still held notes on much of the $675,000 he had sold the team to Frazee and two partners for in 1916. He was now demanding the remainder be paid up. To make matters worse for Frazee, Ruth now had his buddy, Boston drug-gist Johnny Igoe, acting as his "agent." Through Igoe, Babe stated that his old contract calling for a $10,000 salary in 1920 was no longer satisfactory.

He now wanted $20,000 a season and was making his familiar threats not to play unless he got it. Once again there was talk of a boxing career, and with a few awful movie serials under his belt, Ruth also pondered aloud the possibil-ity of becoming a full-time actor. Travel-ing to Los Angeles to play golf, appear in a few paid exhibition games, and make some more movies (although these were mercifully canceled), he had a grand old time spouting to the press while await-ing a concession by his boss.

After the dust settled, Harry Frazee was not a popular man in Boston.

It wasn't to come. Frazee's first love remained the theater, and with his debts to Lannin due, he felt there was no way he could pay what Ruth wanted and continue financing his shows—several of which had recently flopped. Babe's fun-loving dis-regard for such conventions as curfew and normal eating habits could be ignored, but money was another issue. Harry needed help quick.

Enter Yankees owners Jacob Ruppert and Tillinghast Huston. Both were called "Colonel," but other than that and money, the two had little else in common. Huston (a real colonel) had received a modest upbringing in Ohio, then gone off to Cuba and become an officer during the Spanish-American War. He amassed his fortune

Jacob Ruppert was instrumental in bringing the Babe to New York.

working as an engineer on large harbor projects in Havana and other ports but had remained a casual gent and a modest, sloppy dresser who often wore the same suit for days on end. A friend to the ballplayers and sportswriters, who called him "Cap" out of deference to an earlier rank, the big, heavy-set Huston was also a drinking pal of Frazee's—whose New York office was just two doors down from Yankees headquarters. With this in mind, Ruth later speculated in his autobiography that his sale had first been posed by Cap to Harry "over a few glasses of beer."

Ruppert, on the other hand, had been born into money. His grandfather had founded a brewery in Bavaria, and his father made millions plying the same trade in the states. The 51-year-old bachelor was always dressed in the finest suits and shoes, and had his own valet, cook, butler, maid, and laundress on call at his Fifth Avenue apartment. A former four-term congressman from the upper-crust East Side, he was an arrogant self-

This is one of the first shots of the Bambino in his Yankees uniform. Note the length of his bat.

promoter who, after being made an honorary colonel by a New York political crony, insisted on being addressed by the title from then on. He was a collector of fine art, race horses, and—thanks in part to Harry Frazee—an assortment of quality ballplayers. This was the Colonel that Frazee had most often dealt with in past transactions. In fact, Ruppert had supposedly already proposed purchasing Ruth in 1918 following one of Babe's many home runs for Boston at the Polo Grounds.

The Babe explodes out of the box as he hits his 21st homer in 1920. While this one came at the stunning Polo Grounds, he would hit 33 more before the season was over.

The push to get Ruth may also have started with Yankees manager Miller Huggins, a 5'6", 135-pound sparkplug who had piloted the team to third- and fourth-place finishes since coming over from the St. Louis Cardinals. Asked by Ruppert after the 1919 season what the Yanks needed to get over the hump, the rough-edged former big league infielder had supposedly said simply, "Get Ruth from Boston." Apparently he too knew Frazee was hard-up for cash. After being sent to Boston to find out the price tag for the acquisition of Ruth, Huggins returned with news that Frazee would "start talking" at $125,000. Ruppert thought this preposterous, to which Huggins replied, "Bring him to the Polo Grounds and he'll hit 35 homers at least."

Regardless of whoever first proposed it, an offer was put on the table between the Yankees and Red Sox in late December—Ruth straight up for cash. Frazee's decision not to involve any players stemmed partly from his need for quick money and partly from

a conversation he had with Barrow during the negotiations. Calling his manager to a meeting at New York's Knickerbocker Hotel, he told Barrow he intended to sell Ruth but would also get some players in return. "Losing Babe Ruth is bad enough," Barrow remembered telling Frazee. "But don't make it tougher for me by making me show off a lot of 10-cent ballplayers that we got in exchange for him."

Although they were in far better financial shape than Frazee, Ruppert and Huston were leery of spending that much money. They knew that if Ruth joined the club and Yankees attendance increased, Giants manager John McGraw (who liked having the most popular team in town) might get them thrown out of the Polo Grounds and force them to build their own ballpark. There were other things to consider as well. There was the looming threat of Prohibition, slated to go into effect a few weeks later on January 16, 1920. A major source of Ruppert's income came from the 1.3 million barrels of beer his brewery produced each year, and he figured to have far less capital to work with once the new law banning the purchase, consumption, or transportation of alcohol within the United States went into effect.

Despite their apprehensions, Ruppert and Huston apparently knew one thing: This was too good a chance to pass up. On December 26, 1919, unbeknownst to the public, a deal was struck in which Frazee would be paid $25,000 up front for Ruth, along with three promissory notes of $25,000 each. Harry would also receive a loan of $300,000 against the mortgage at Fenway Park, making the final deal worth

$400,000—nearly the full amount Ruppert and Huston had paid for the entire Yankees franchise just four years before. The $100,000 in cash was easily the most ever paid for a ballplayer, doubling the $50,000 the Indians had given the Red Sox for Tris Speaker in 1916. Fans were still kept in the dark, but the first hint that something was awry came when Frazee told reporters the next day he was willing to accept offers for any player on Boston's roster but one—outfielder Harry Hooper.

Huggins was sent to Los Angeles to alert Ruth of the still-secret deal and take care of Babe's contract demands. Meeting up with his newest ballplayer on the Griffith Park golf course, he introduced himself and shook hands. Ruth later admitted he already had a feeling at this point he had been traded, but he made small talk until Huggins got around to asking how he'd feel about playing for the Yankees. "I'm happy with the Red Sox," Babe replied. "I like Boston. But if Frazee sends me to the Yankees, I'll play as hard for them as I did for him."

Next, Huggins laid down the law. "Babe, you've been a pretty wild boy in Boston. In New York you'll have to behave. You'll have to be strictly business." The strait-laced manager went on to warn of the dangers and temptations that could be found in New York, dangers and temptations that no player on his team should succumb to under any circumstances. The approach Huggins took irked the usually fun-loving Ruth, who after listening in boredom for a while shot back, "I already told you I'll play the best I can. Let's get down to business. How much are you going to pay me?"

As per Ruppert's instructions, Huggins offered first $15,000 and then $17,500 a year. Ruth restated his original $20,000 demand, then

Diminutive manager Miller Huggins tried in vain to curb the nocturnal habits of the fun-loving Babe.

threw in that he also expected part of the profits Frazee had received for his sale. Huggins ran the numbers by Ruppert, and at their next meeting Babe signed a contract that satisfied both parties. Ruth would be paid $10,000 for each of the next two seasons—his 1919 salary—but would also receive an immediate bonus of $1,000 and $20,000 more paid out over the two-year period in $2,500 intervals. The numbers added up to $20,500 each season—more even than Cobb—and Ruth supposedly promised to behave himself while earning it.

Huggins wired word of the signing back to Ruppert, and late on the Monday afternoon of January 5, 1920, Frazee made the deal public with a press conference

With the acquisition of the mighty Bambino, New York—and baseball—would never be the same.

in Boston. "The price was something enormous, but I do not care to name the figures," Harry told reporters. "It was an amount the club could not afford to refuse. I should have preferred to have taken players in exchange for Ruth, but no club would have given me the equivalent in men without wrecking itself, and so the deal had to be made on a cash basis. No other club could afford to give the amount the Yankees have paid for him, and I do not mind saying I think they are taking a gamble. While Ruth is undoubtedly the greatest hitter the game has ever seen, he is likewise one of the most selfish and inconsiderate men ever to put on a baseball uniform."

Frazee went on to cite Ruth as the reason for Boston's poor showing the previous season, stating that "you will notice that a one-man team is almost invariably in the second division. . . . The other players have little incentive or encouragement for great effort when the spectators can see only one man in the game and so the one man has an upsetting influence on the others." Frazee was actually *blaming* Babe for being a great player on a bad team. As his ridiculous rambling continued, he spoke of Ruth's greed in seeking a new contract and how his "insubordination" had "endangered the discipline of the whole squad."

There was a promise from Frazee that he would use the money from the sale to purchase quality ballplayers, but the now-leery Boston fans, after watching their once-perennial champions slowly dismantled by the smooth-talking owner, didn't buy it. The transaction was front-page news in all the city's newspapers that evening, and most of the reaction was negative. The *Boston Post* called the move "a tremendous blow to the army of loyal fans" and predicted the Sox would be "crowding the Athletics for eighth place in 1920." Another paper featured a cartoon showing historic Faneuil Hall and the Boston Public Library adorned with "For Sale" signs. Apparently the artist felt no local landmark was safe with Harry Frazee in town, and Red Sox fans from all walks of life voiced their agreement with some prophetic judgements.

"Ruth was 90 percent of our club last summer," said Johnny Keenan, leader of the "Royal Rooters" fan club that had been cheering and serenading the Red Sox at home games through most of the team's existence. "It will be impossible to replace the strength Ruth gave the Sox." A Knights of Columbus chapter in South Boston adopted a resolution declaring, "It is the consensus of opinion in K of C circles that Boston fans were dealt unfairly in the sale of Brother Ruth, and it is felt that commercialism is fast gaining control over baseball." Upon seeing a poster near Fenway park adver-

While this birch is bigger than his usual weapon of choice, the Babe proves he really can swing the lumber.

tising Frazee's current show running in Boston—*My Lady Friends*—one disgruntled fan was heard to comment, "Those are the only friends that blankety-blank has."

Yankees rooters were understandably more excited. Ruth was known as a notorious pull hitter, and in the Polo Grounds, the right field foul line stood just 257 feet from home plate. Babe had hit five of his first 11 big league homers in the park, and Huggins's prediction of 35 homers for Ruth over an entire season there seemed a good estimate. A group of New York sportswriters gathered to toast the city's good

fortune and their own pending great copy, but *The New York Times* thought the whole business rather shady. It was a poor state of affairs, an editorial in the paper surmised, when a good player on a weak team could hold out "for an imposing salary" and "get somebody in New York or Chicago to buy his services." Running under the headline "The High Price of Home Runs," the editorial went on to compare Ruth's salary to that of a Columbia University professor.

Fenway Park is one of the few baseball venues that has remained virtually unchanged from the days of Ruth.

Amidst this exciting backdrop came several salvos from sunny California and the Babe Ruth camp—some true and many fictional. "'Babe' Says He Will Play in Boston or Nowhere" one *Globe* sub-headline read, with Igoe claiming to have received a telegram from Ruth reading: "Will not play anywhere but Boston. Will leave for the East Monday." It was an odd message considering Ruth had already agreed to terms with Huggins, and a day later Babe seemingly admitted his fate when he wired to Igoe: "Tell the newspapermen that I am sorry to be traded to New York and hate to get away from Boston fans." Ruth still claimed he would return to town soon, but now only to refute Frazee's disparaging remarks and hopefully pocket some dough from his sale.

When Ruth did come to Boston in mid-January, Frazee refused to meet him. Babe said the owner was simply trying to "alibi himself with the fans" and revealed that when given his "day" the previous September he had received only a cigar from tightwad Harry while his wife, Helen, was forced to pay her own way into Fenway. He also defended his demand for a higher salary: "Any fair-minded fan knows that my efforts on the Boston club last season warranted a much higher salary and I asked for it," Ruth said. "I have always hustled as much as any man on the diamond." Folks accepted the words as sincere; Boston fans never viewed Ruth as a greedy ballplayer, and for the rest of his career he would be looked upon as a hero in the city where his fame began.

The same could not be said of Harry Frazee. He had given away baseball's single most spectacular performer—a figure whose feats were changing the very nature of the game—and had received not *one* ballplayer in return. The money he did get kept him going so he could finance more shows, and eventually his luck turned back around. *Madame Sherry* netted more than a half million dollars, and in 1925 Harry really hit it big with *No, No, Nanette*—the play that made "Tea for Two" famous and earned him more than $2.5 million during its worldwide run.

Bostonians saw it as blood money. By this time Frazee had sold off Boston's remaining quality players to Ruppert and Huston and was mercifully out of baseball. Following the Ruth deal had come moves sending Wally Shang, Waite Hoyt, Everett Scott, Joe Bush, Sam Jones, Joe Dugan, and Herb Pennock to New York for mostly cash and a few worthless bodies. When the Yankees won their first World Series in 1923, playing in brand-new Yankee Stadium ("The House That Ruth Built"), they did so with 11 players who had once worn a Red Sox uniform. Over one million fans cheered on Boston's former heroes

Waite Hoyt, another product of the Frazee fallout, found himself teaming up with Babe again in New York.

In the bright lights of New York, the Babe's on-field persona had real marketing appeal.

in New York that summer, while back at Fenway the "Dead" Sox drew under 230,000.

All told, the Yankees won seven AL pennants and four World Series during Ruth's 15 seasons with the club, enough to build a powerful farm system that would eventually produce 29 league and 20 world championships in the first 54 years following what would be, for Bostonians at least, the worst transaction in baseball history. The Yankees earned an almost mythical reputation as the greatest dynasty in professional sports, while the Red Sox . . . well, the Red Sox became the team that continues to break the hearts of fans.

After winning five of the first 15 modern World Series, the victims of Frazee's greed saw their fortunes continue to slide following Ruth's departure. Boston finished fifth the next two seasons, last in 1922, and then rose above seventh place just once through 1933. Their average record the first 14 seasons without Babe was 54-95, and during one eight-year period they never finished closer than 43½ games to first place. The Yankees made over $3½ million from 1920 to '30; the Red Sox were the only major-league team to lose money over the span.

Things improved after owner Tom Yawkey arrived in '33 and began stocking the team with stars like Joe Cronin, Bobby Doerr, and Ted Williams, but when Boston again became an American League power, one team always seemed to stand between them and a pennant—the New York Yankees. It wasn't until 1946 that a Red Sox team returned to the World Series, but that and three subsequent trips brought the same result—a loss in seven games.

Several other agonizing near misses in the regular and postseason helped earn the team that had gone 5-0 in World Series competition through 1918 a reputation as baseball's biggest chokers, and imaginative Fenway faithful came up with their own excuse for the rotten luck. Since the Yankees so often seemed at the heart of their problems, it was felt that Babe Ruth must be sending bad vibes toward his former club from the grave. The "Curse of the Bambino" has never been proven, but some rather creative measures have been undertaken or suggested to stop it—exorcisms, prayers from clergymen, and the buying back of Ruth's contract among them. Entering the 1995 season, none had worked.

Whether or not the Red Sox are cursed, the mere mention of Harry Frazee or *No, No, Nanette* still causes New England baseball fans to cringe. Yankees followers, however, seem just fine on the subject. As far as they're concerned, Ruppert and Huston's "gamble" worked out quite nicely.

Ruth bypassed New York on his trip home from California, and it was only after getting Helen settled in on the farm outside Boston that he got his first taste of the Big Apple. Meeting up on February 28 with the rest of the Yankees contingent at Pennsylvania Station just a few minutes before their sleeper train was to depart for Florida and spring training, he was besieged by what was then an uncommon sight away from the ballpark—hordes of fans begging for handshakes and autographs.

The Babe and a trio of his youthful admires prepare to take a spin.

Putting down his golf clubs, a happy and somewhat surprised Ruth obliged. The moment marked a turning point in his life. For the rest of his career, especially while in New York, Babe would have to grow used to sharing time in public with his many admirers. Many ballplayers looked down at the task, thinking it an undesirable chore.

Along with the Bambino's athletic ability, he was able to become such a marketing prototype because of his genuine public relations skills.

Ruth received more requests than anyone, yet few were as generous with their time or as naturally warm toward fans. He seemed to have a constant urge to see others happy, perhaps stemming from his own neglected, unsatisfying upbringing. As he came to share his smile and good fortune with others, it was children who always received the most attention. No matter how turbulent his own life got, he always found time for kids. This as much as anything else contributed so positively to his growing legend.

Babe's first moments with Yankees teammates marked a sharp contrast to the frustrating experiences he had encountered as a Red Sox rookie six years before. Friendly center fielder Frank "Ping" Bodie introduced him all around, although Ruth already knew most of the players on the team. Introductions never meant much to the Babe anyway. He had an awful time with names, probably more out of a lack of necessity than conceit or ignorance. He encountered so many people in his varied travels who were simply glad to meet him that he likely found it made more sense not to bother with such formalities. Teammates were no exception.

Many who played with Ruth for several years later claimed without the slightest hint of anger that he never knew their real names, the most famous case of all probably being that of Waite Hoyt. A Hall of Fame pitcher and teammate of Ruth's for 11 years in Boston and New York, Hoyt had just found out he had been traded to the Tigers during the 1930 season when Babe approached him. Looking at the friend who had won over 160 games in their decade-plus together, Ruth stuck out his hand and said warmly, "Good bye, Walter." If Hoyt was bothered by the incident, he never let on. Like most comrades of the Babe, he was forever retelling such stories to enraptured audiences for the rest of his life.

Handed his first $5 for expense money as the train headed to Jacksonville, Ruth was quick to urge his new mates to get a card game going. One of his sidelines in Boston had been an interest in a cigar factory that produced the "Babe Ruth Cigar," and he had plenty to hand around on the trip south. Ruth was up to his old clowning ways when the club arrived in Florida and began practice. This time, he was greeted with a very different response to his antics. In fact, the reaction again showed how far he had come since his first days in Boston. One day early in camp, Babe was working out at third base, and Bodie cut in front of him for a grounder. Yelling in mock protest, Ruth picked up his 5'8", 195-pound roommate, turned him upside down, plopped him down on the grass, and sat on him. This time there were no angry words or fisticuffs like Babe's rookie shenanigans toward Joe Wood had brought on. This time, there was only laughter.

In the past a single sportswriter had often dispatched Yankees stories to several New York papers during spring training, but now every paper wanted exclusive stories on the daily doings of the Babe. In fact, 13 reporters wound up in Florida, probably the most to

Before he even arrived in New York, the Bambino had learned his name had marketability. Here he passes out "Babe Ruth Cigars" on February 12, 1920.

ever cover one team in training camp up until that time. They promptly went to work. Even before the games started, such legendary scribes as Fred Lieb, Damon Runyon, and Sid Mercer were cranking out copy that appeared under such headlines as "Ruth Complains of Indigestion," "Ruth's Big Bats Arrive in Camp," and "Ruth a Fizzle on Links; Home Run King Smashes Several Clubs." Even a succinct run-down of Ruth's conquests at the dinner table one evening was deemed worthy of a feature story, and the readers ate it up.

Ping Bodie was not fast, but he was quick-witted. It was after Bodie's failed stolen base attempt that columnist Bugs Baer wrote, "There was larceny in his heart, but his feet were honest."

The Jacksonville Chamber of Commerce had also geared up for Babe's arrival, publicizing each Yankee exhibition game throughout Florida as a chance for fans to see baseball's greatest new star. The New York team itself was not much of an attraction; the Yankees had never won a pennant, and despite the great players acquired from Frazee, they were not yet known as the regal and imposing club they would soon become. Ruth was the draw, and the club performed before record crowds throughout the spring.

At first Babe seemed to have trouble living up to the billing. He started slowly in camp, and after striking out several times a game during a series with the Brooklyn Dodgers, he was bothered by spiteful comments and headlines in the newspapers back East. One day a fan was continuously riding the struggling outfielder from the stands, and Babe eventually snapped. He climbed into the seats in pursuit of the insult artist ("Ruth Turns on Blatant Fan Who Calls Him a 'Piece of Cheese'"), and the man pulled out a knife which Ruth later recalled looked "about a foot long."

Someone intervened before either could get hurt. "I believe it was the very next day that I got going," Ruth said in his autobiography. Following a mammoth home run on April 1, he was indeed among the team's hottest hitters the remainder of camp.

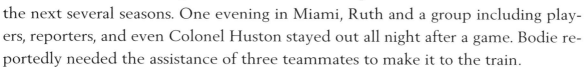

Off the field, Babe seemed intent on doing everything Huggins had warned against during their first meeting. Ruth's reputation for mischief was growing as fast as his popularity, and Bodie grew accustomed to taking both his own suitcase and Babe's to their hotel room each time the Yankees train reached a new town. Barely waiting until the wheels stopped rolling, Ruth was off in search of whatever the town had to offer, a ritual teammates would grow to view as commonplace the next several seasons. One evening in Miami, Ruth and a group including players, reporters, and even Colonel Huston stayed out all night after a game. Bodie reportedly needed the assistance of three teammates to make it to the train.

Ping Bodie's roommate, the most famous suitcase in baseball.

Ruth was not much better off. He later admitted that "my reflexes were a bit off that day," and while in pursuit of a fly ball that afternoon ran directly into a palm

tree—knocking himself cold. He was back to his old tricks soon thereafter, and it was around this time that the famous remark that most aptly summed up Ruth's social life began making the rounds. Later historians would give credit to Bodie or a number of other teammates, but the line could have come from anybody. Asked what it was like to share quarters with the wild young star, Bodie had answered, "I don't room with Ruth. I room with his suitcase."

Bodie wouldn't be rooming with anybody on the club for a while, as he jumped the team in March due to personal problems. Another out-

Ruth had his share of run-ins with Miller Huggins but eventually learned to respect his skipper.

fielder, Chick Fewster, was hit in the head by a pitch and after heading north to Baltimore for surgery was all but finished for the season. The club's fly-catching corps thus depleted, Ruth asked Huggins if he could play center field and not "get myself all smashed up going after a fly ball" in the short left and right field walls of the Polo Grounds. Huggins obliged by putting Babe in center for opening day in Philadelphia, and Ruth promptly dropped a fly ball in the eighth that allowed the last-place Athletics to score twice and capture the game. He was soon back in right, where he remained virtually the rest of his career.

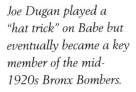

It was an embarrassing debut, but Babe handled both the incident and its aftermath well. The day following the miscue, A's third baseman Joe Dugan had a little trick to play on his future teammate; a messenger was sent out to home plate with a package while Ruth was at bat, and when Babe opened it he found a brown derby inside. In those days, such a hat was a symbol of ineptitude. Umpires and fellow players laughed at Babe's gift. Everyone present awaited a Ruth-like outburst, but what came instead was a grin, wave, and tip of the derby to adoring fans. The Babe was continuing to learn what the public wanted from him and seemed to know just how to respond.

Joe Dugan played a "hat trick" on Babe but eventually became a key member of the mid-1920s Bronx Bombers.

Hall of Famer Herb Pennock was another ballplayer who moved from Boston to the Bronx.

The games themselves were once again proving a struggle. Ruth had two weak singles in the opener at Philadelphia, struck out three times the following day, and did little of note as the Yanks were swept three straight by the Red Sox in Boston. It was hoped a return to the Polo Grounds would do the Babe good, but he pulled a muscle in his rib cage during batting practice and then again after striking out in the first inning. He left the game to

the loud displeasure of a packed home crowd and didn't return for several days. Through all of April (11 games), he failed to hit a home run. Huggins's prediction of 35 homers was beginning to look like a joke.

Appropriately, the Red Sox were at the center of the action when Babe finally gave his manager and New Yorkers what they had been anxiously awaiting. Boston was a surprising 10-2 and in first place when they came to town May 1, but in the second game of the series Ruth hit a tremendous home run off Herb Pennock over the Polo Grounds roof—even far-ther than his record-breaking 28th homer had traveled in the same park the previous September. The moment marked the beginning of New York's march out of the sec-ond division and the start of Frazee's fabulous flops toward it. The Yankees swept the series (Babe homering the next day as well), and Ruth was on his way to the most fantastic season in mod-ern baseball history.

The Sultan heads home after his 22nd swat in 1920.

Babe made up for his homerless April with 12 in May, including a stretch late in the month when he hit six in six days—three of them against the Red Sox at Fen-way Park. The crowds at the Polo Grounds continued to grow, and some 15,000 were turned away on Sunday, May 16 when a record 38,600 packed the place and forced police to shut down ticket windows. June brought another 12 homers—in-cluding three in a doubleheader versus Washington on June 2—and Babe began a consecutive-game hitting streak that eventually reached 26 games before being snapped in mid-July. On July 11, his average stood at .385.

Here was an example of another aspect of Ruth's game that has been eroded somewhat—his ability to hit for a consistently high average. For some, the image comes to mind of the Babe as an all-or-nothing free swinger at the plate. While this

Babe Ruth: His Life and Times

In his Boston days, and when he first came to New York, Ruth cut a dashing figure—down to his undergarments.

is how he had been depicted in some less-than-accurate film versions of his life story, it just isn't true. He did swing mightier than most, but his .342 lifetime batting average (including a high of .393) indicates he was far from undisciplined at the plate. His stance seemed to resemble that of fellow left-handed batter Joe Jackson. There was obviously something in the stance that worked for both sluggers. Jackson, as one may recall, was the great left fielder whose involvement in the "Black Sox" scandal would lead to his banishment. Joe's .356 career average remains the third-highest of all-time, and Ruth called him "the greatest natural hitter I have ever seen."

Jackson's success came from a stance in which he stood with his feet 20 inches apart, put the bulk of his weight on his rear left foot, and aimed his right shoulder at the pitcher—resulting in an almost propeller-like motion as he swung. Babe altered things somewhat by keeping his feet just eight to nine inches apart, which gave him even a quicker pivot to work from, but it also made it nearly impossible to check a swing. Beginning his upward cut with his back almost to the pitcher, he would twist around as the ball came in, giving his wrist an extra twist just as he made contact.

Of course, that was providing he made contact. The result of his unorthodox stance was that many Ruth at bats ended with a cross-legged Babe curled up pretzel-like and the victim of another strikeout, but even the mighty misses thrilled fans. "Throughout his career of twenty years, Ruth never changed the basics of that gorgeous, gargantuan arc—a swing that fascinated the crowd as much as the personality of the man behind it," wrote legendary sportswriter Grantland Rice. "To watch Ruth go down swinging, often sprawling

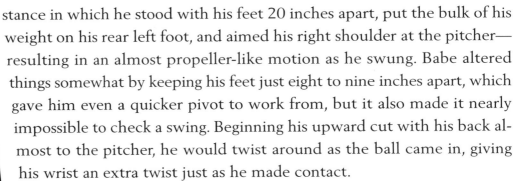

from the violence of his cut, was almost as exciting as seeing him blast one out of the park."

Ruth seemed to play up the all-or-nothing image himself. "Once my swing starts, I can't change it or pull up on it," he said. "It's all or nothing." Despite its appearances, this was a precise swing that had taken hard work to master. Ruth's great eyesight, timing, and co-ordination (again, despite the stereotypes) enabled him to alter his grip or stance however much was necessary to hit the ball at full force. He could bunt and hit to the opposite field when the need arose, and nobody could remember another hitter who chose not to choke up on the bat with two strikes. It didn't matter whether the pitch was at his knees or armpits; Babe seemed to find a way to power it on a long, arching drive out of the park.

Other batters may have hit the ball harder (a perfect example being future teammate Gehrig), but nobody hit it as far or as high. Of the first 16 homers Ruth hit at the Polo Grounds in 1920, all reached the second deck or left the park completely. It was said that Babe hit infield pops so high he was often at second base before they were caught. The prodigious power was helped by a 42- to 46-ounce bat, at least a pound heavier than the average stick used by major leaguers. "Home runs executed by Babe Ruth are not mere home runs," wrote W.O. McGeehan of the *New York Herald-Tribune*. "Each home run seems to possess an individuality and eccentricities of its own. After the game the multitudes linger in the lot to trace the path taken by the ball."

The Babe's mighty grip and position of his feet sustain the fallacy that he was an all-or-nothing batsman.

Ruth's feats at the plate, of course, were only half the story. Babe moved Helen down from Boston, and the couple took up residence in a sumptuous suite within the elegant Astonia Hotel on Broadway. Among the building's residents were famous musicians, writers, and politicians. Ruth, however, was soon claiming bigger headlines than any of his esteemed neighbors with a social life that rivaled that of a movie star. He met many of the Hollywood gentry, in fact, and here again his difficulty with names made for a great story. Asked by a teammate where he had been one night, Babe spoke of attending "a party with those movie people." Asked which movie people, he replied, "Oh, you know, what the hell are their names?" Apparently Douglas Fairbanks and Mary Pickford—the reigning stars of the silver screen of their day—were no more memorable than Waite Hoyt.

While Helen Ruth wasn't drawn into the lure of fast times and big city life, the Babe seemed to thrive on it. They inevitably began to drift apart.

Even if he didn't remember them, whoever met Ruth seemed to enjoy the experience. The admirers ranged from everyday people on the street to the bootleggers, politicians, and stars of stage and screen he encountered in the speakeasies of Manhattan. The only one who didn't seem impressed was Helen; she surely knew of his vicissitudes on the road and never took to the fishbowl life which Babe thrived. The encounters with reporters and cameramen that accosted the couple each time they left the apartment led to nightmares and bouts of depression. To help escape from the onslaught of press, Helen began spending more and more time by herself back on the Sudbury farm.

If Ruth was bothered by this event, he didn't let it show. His car accident in Boston had apparently had no affect on his thrill for speed, and he continued to purchase customized, powerful automobiles and then promptly wreck them or get caught for speeding. He routinely ignored stoplights and traffic signals on the drive from the Astonia to the Polo Grounds, but police usually let him go with a smile. On July 20, however, throwing caution to the wind nearly cost him his life.

Taking his newest car on a Yankee road trip to Philadelphia and Washington, Ruth was driving late one night just outside rural Wawa, Pennsylvania, with Helen and three friends from the club. When he sped dangerously around a curve, the auto skidded out of control. As the machine went off the road, Helen and coach Charley O'Leary were thrown clear as it flipped over.

Crawling from the wreck, Ruth found his wife in fine health but O'Leary looking unconscious and dead. "Oh God, bring Charley back. I didn't mean it," Babe cried, and O'Leary did in fact turn out to be okay. The car was another story, and after walking to a nearby farm and spending the night, the group returned to the crash site accompanied by a mechanic. "Sell it," Ruth supposedly said of the wreck. "Take whatever you can get for it. I'm through with it." Leaving the stunned mechanic and his free parts supply behind, Babe's party proceeded on to Philadelphia. "RUTH REPORTEDLY KILLED IN CAR CRASH" was the headline they found in one local paper, but Babe was supposedly well enough to purchase a new version of the identical car when he returned to New York.

Babe did suffer a banged-up knee in the mishap, one of many injuries that plagued him his first year with the Yankees. In addition to the pulled muscle in April there was a strained leg in May, a bout of the flu the same month, a jammed wrist suffered while sliding in July, and an infection on his right forearm in August. The last was initially brought on by an insect sting, which Ruth infected by trying to treat it himself with "instruments" found at home.

He missed a total of 12 games for his various ills, but with the way he was living, it was incredible he didn't spend more time sidelined. In addition to his nearly nightly escapades throughout New York, he spent part of August motoring back and forth between the Bronx and Fort Lee, New Jersey, to make a silent

Put it here, I dare ya! The Sultan prepares to knock the cover off one.

Fans couldn't get enough of the gregarious slugger. With his tremendous appeal, the Babe would find himself on many more covers in the future.

Scenes from Headin' Home, *not exactly one of the Babe's bigger hits.*

The Babe seemed to show up everywhere, getting the kind of media coverage usually reserved for royalty.

film comedy about (imagine this) a young baseball slugger who hits homers and wins the girl. He missed about a week of batting practice working on *Headin' Home* and often showed up at the ballpark coated in face makeup. He made $15,000 for the cliché-ridden catastrophe, but $35,000 more was lost in a check that he failed to cash until after the production company had already folded a few months later.

Babe sued another company for $250,000 after they took footage of him batting and turned it into a series of instructional films, but the judge threw the case out, declaring that Ruth was so popular a figure he could be photographed without permission. He had officially become a phenomenon. Even if he hadn't mastered acting, his services were being rapidly sought for endorsements. One of these came from Republican campaign managers, who upon discovering Ty Cobb had voiced support for Democratic presidential candidate James Cox wanted Babe to meet their own Warren Harding during his "front-porch" campaign. Ruth refused initially, but put his affiliations aside on being informed he'd receive $4,000 for his trouble. The Yankee schedule and other circumstances kept him from ever making it to Ohio, however, and Ruth (who never voted himself until 1944) lost out on the dough.

Even the campaign often seemed to take a backseat to Ruth's exploits in the newspapers. In the days before television and radio brought baseball into nearly every home (the first radio broadcast of a game came just that summer), reporters continued to follow his every move with stories and "Babe Ruth Boxes." These tidbits about the Babe even went so far as to document his weight and daily diet. "Babe Ruth is a bigger show this year than baseball itself," a *New York Sun* writer surmised. "The infant heads a procession whenever he walks around. They bring their babies to the park and point him out. And the hand that shook the hand of Babe Ruth is looked upon with quite as much awe as the hand that shook the hand of John L. Sullivan (the great bare-handed boxing champ) used to be."

Unlike the trashy tabloid treatment people in the public eye are subjected to today, any negative information was often sugar-coated or left out altogether. In an era when reporters and players traveling on the train together formed lifelong friendships, the private lives of athletes were largely kept out of print; the fans seemed content with play-by-play and the lighter side of the game, and nobody drew more fluff in the daily papers than Ruth. He quickly earned a wealth of nicknames from admiring scribes thankful for colorful copy—the Sultan of Swat, the Bambino, the Maharajah of Mash—and throughout morning, evening, and late editions the praise kept coming. "He was a special case," remembered Shirley Povich of the *Washington Post* seven decades later. "Everybody knew what contributions he was making to the game, and what would have been exposed in this later day of baseball writing was simply ignored in those times."

What more could a sailor on leave hope for than a day at the ballpark and a chance to meet the Bambino.

His power and flamboyant style were impossible to ignore and appealed to post-war Americans earning more money than ever and seeking new ways to spend it. The puritan barriers of the past were being broken down as the nation became increasingly urbanized; women were given the vote in 1920, the radio was slowly replacing the Victrola as the major source of family entertainment, and despite the passage of prohibition more and more young people were living fast and drinking hard. It seemed only appropriate baseball should undergo its own radical change, and when it did Ruth was the catalyst. His slugging fit right into this transition, symbolizing the fast-moving dreams of the Jazz Age.

Bob Meusel and the Babe filled the third and fourth spots in the batting order, often resulting in a headache for the opposing pitcher.

The fans just couldn't get enough of him. July 9 was declared "Babe Ruth Day" at the Polo Grounds, and after receiving a diamond-studded watch fob from a local Knights of Columbus chapter, the honoree homered and tipped his cap to the presenters while rounding the bases. Huge crowds met the Yankees in every park around the league, including record throngs in five of the seven AL cities. The fans ranged from small children to great-grandfathers, but all wanted the same thing: to see Babe hit one out. He had become quite the showman on the field of play.

In St. Louis, three cowboys approached Babe in the Yankee locker room, telling him of how they had ridden on horseback three days to reach a Wyoming railroad station and a train headed for Missouri. "Baby Ruth," one supposedly told him, "I'd have ridden on horseback all the way to St. Louis to see you hit them home runs." One Washington man apparently took the excitement a bit too far and dropped dead of a heart attack following a Ruth homer. The thrill of seeing the Bambino also held an immense and universal appeal for children across the land. Wherever he went, Babe seemed to be surrounded by kids.

Pitchers were booed by their home crowds when they walked the visiting batsman, but this appeared to be the only way to stop him. Many of Ruth's bases on balls were intentional, although this was not yet a recorded statistic. When this practice increased later in the season, Huggins attempted to stop the trend by moving Babe from fourth to third in the order and placing young slugger Bob Meusel at cleanup. The results were often mixed. On July 11, Ruth homered against Howard Ehmke of Detroit but in three other at bats was walked on four straight pitches. In the course of the entire game, he swung the bat twice.

Even when Ruth failed to get many licks, the Yankees proved capable of winning. The addition of Mays to the pitching staff (where the right-hander quickly became the ace) had given the team an exceptional four-man rotation that also included 20-game winner Bob Shawkey (the AL ERA champ), Jack Quinn, and Rip Collins. Ernie Shore was still around for a spot start when needed. First base-man Wally Pipp was one of the league's most consistent batsmen, Muddy Ruel a promising catcher, and steady Del Pratt, Roger Peckinpaugh, and Aaron Ward rounded out the infield. Bodie (back from his brief hiatus) and Duffy Lewis were veteran out-fielders; Meusel, a powerful rookie, provided the club with its second most danger-ous power hitter. Before Ruth even joined the team, the starting lineup had been dubbed "Murderer's Row" by a newspaper cartoonist.

There didn't seem to be anything that the Babe couldn't pitch.

Still, Babe far outshined them all. On July 15, he tied his record of 29 home runs with a blast at the Polo Grounds off Bill Burwell of St. Louis and four days later set a new record three times with a trio of shots in a doubleheader against the White

Sox. He had 37 homers through July, and these feats plus an ex-tremely tight American League pennant race between New York, Chicago, and the Cleveland Indians helped the Yankees draw nearly 200,000—an unheard-of figure—during a seven-game homestand late in the month. The battle stayed close through the ensuing weeks. When the Indians visited New York for a three-game series starting on

Ruth and Ping Bodie, both a couple of hams, check out some breakfast options.

First baseman Wally Pipp was one of the league's most consistent batsmen.

Monday, August 16, they were only four percentage points ahead of Chicago and a half game in front of the Yanks.

A soft rain fell early on, and Cleveland held a 3-0 lead when Indians shortstop Ray Chapman stepped up to face Mays leading off the fifth inning. Leaning over the plate in his usual crouched stance, Ray took a ball and then awaited Mays's second offering.

Throwing out of the underhand windup that had already carried him to an 18-8 record, Mays delivered a fastball high and inside that seemed to paralyze Chapman. It struck Ray in the left temple so hard that when it bounced toward the pitcher, backstop Muddy Ruel picked it up and fired it to first, thinking he had made the first out of the inning. When Chapman fell sort of in a sitting/sprawling position inside the batter's box with blood oozing from his ear, Ruel knew something was wrong. A doctor was then summoned from the stands.

As Ruth watched from the outfield, Chapman managed to get to his feet. Unable to speak, he was brought to the visitor's clubhouse at the Polo Grounds. The doctor determined emergency surgery would be necessary to relieve pressure on his brain. There was still baseball to be played, and it wasn't until after the Yankees missed their chance to take over first place in the standings with a 4-3 loss that

Ray Chapman suffered an untimely demise on the ball field.

the players were told Chapman had been taken to St. Lawrence hospital. Doctors operated later that night, but at 4:40 the next morning, Chapman died of an intercranial hemorrhage. He was the first (and thankfully the only) major leaguer killed by a pitch.

The Babe was happy to help St. Mary's when the opportunity arose.

The Yankees postponed Tuesday afternoon's game, then split two 4-3 contests (Ruth slugging his 43rd homer) to remain one and a half games out. Opposing players and sportswriters began calling for the banishment of Mays—who already had a reputation for scuffing up balls and pitching tight—but he stayed with the club and won eight games down the stretch to help New York briefly take over first. Ruth also rebounded from hitting just six August homers to hit 10 homers over his final 24 games, marking one of the best power surges of his career. Regardless of the Babe's efforts, however, the Yankees stumbled on their final western swing. When all was said and done, they would finish three games back.

The Bambino was a marketing dream come true.

Even in defeat, however, there was some fun in store for the final days of the campaign as the Yankees were accompanied on their last roadtrips by Brother Matthias and a band comprised of youngsters from St. Mary's. The boys were hoping to raise money to rebuild the institution after a ravaging fire in April 1919. When Ruth arranged to have them come along to Cleveland, Detroit, and Chicago, the school netted over $13,000 in donations. Babe did his part by contributing $4,100 (a fifth of his salary) to the cause and routinely pleasing photographers by wielding a tuba and posing with the group.

Singing the Babe's praises, this sheet music dates from 1919.

It was a colorful way to end a stupendous summer. A Yankee pennant would have to wait at least another year despite a franchise-best 95-59 record, but New York's baseball revolution had already begun. Just how dominating was Ruth's season? His final tally of 54 home runs was higher than the total of 14 of 15 other major league *teams* (the Phillies had 64). All told, he stroked one of every seven homers hit in the AL that year. League runner-up George Sisler had just 19 homers; National League champ Cy Williams a mere 15. In fact, only 15 major leaguers hit as many as 10 homers that season. Far more than even in his incredible 1919 season, Babe had set power standards the likes of which baseball had never seen.

His other numbers were similarly imposing. He led the AL with 137 RBI and 158 runs, hit .376 (fourth in the league), and had 36 doubles, nine triples, and 14 stolen bases (further proof there was a strong, intelligent athlete at work). His slugging percentage of .847 set a major league record, and no other player has ever come within 75 points of the mark. The banishment of the "spitball" and other trick pitches was cited as a reason for Ruth's fantastic success, along with unsubstantiated rumors of a "juiced up" ball that saw league averages rise dramatically over the previous year.

A photo opportunity. Mayor Thompson of Chicago receives a bat from Ruth.

In reality, what he did went beyond explanation. For the crowds that packed the Polo Grounds all year, the reasons didn't matter anyway. They simply loved what they were seeing, and the Yankees wound up more than doubling their attendance. In fact, they drew a major league record 1,289,422 fans, becoming the first team to ever go over one million. Seven other major league teams set attendance records on the season, much of the credit going to Ruth. In

Just like he was fond of doing with baseballs, the Babe squashes the stuffing out of Lou Archer on the set of Babe Comes Home, one of the Bambino's film endeavors.

an era of giants like Ty Cobb, Walter Johnson, and Tris Speaker, the Babe was the most popular player in the game and the biggest drawing card in all of sports.

Thinking himself no longer quite so naive, Ruth was ready to capitalize on his popularity. He earned several thousand dollars in a series of exhibition games following the season, then signed on with John McGraw for a barnstorming tour of Cuba with a team comprised mostly of Giants players. He took Helen along for the trip and made anywhere from $25,000 to $40,000 for the games. However, when he discovered he liked the excitement of putting money on the nose of a horse, he ended up tossing at least that much away. Varying accounts intimate that he was set up by swindlers claiming "insider information," but whatever the case Babe enjoyed himself. He weighed 240 pounds by the time he came home and was ready to take up right where he left off in the spring.

Ruth was out to prove the season had not been a fluke—only a beginning.

1921-1925

The Roaring Twenties:
Big Bats and Bellyaches

With vim and verve
he walloped the curve
From Texas to Duluth.
Which is no small task,
And I rise to ask:
Was there ever a guy like Ruth?

—John Kieran, sports author

THE ROARING TWENTIES: BIG BATS AND BELLYACHES

Previous page: Dorothy Ruth and her famous daddy don matching hats while spending a day in the great outdoors.

*A*lthough the Yankees failed to win the 1920 American League flag, it certainly hadn't been Ruth's fault. Taking advantage of the improved baseball-making technology that had tightened the ball's core, Ruth's offensive stats for that season have been called the greatest individual offensive performance of any player ever. Baseball, traumatized by the September beaning death of Cleveland infielder Ray Chapman, made rule changes before the 1921 season that had the effect of making the ball even livelier: Pitches that involved defacing the baseball (meaning everything from spitballs to emery pitches) were banned, and once a ball got dirty it had to be removed from the game.

The Babe would delight in banging the bright, shiny new balls all over the place, putting up even bigger numbers than in 1920, and the Yankees would reach the World Series for the first time in their history. Soon after this feat, though, Babe would find himself locked into a career-threatening battle with possibly the only person in baseball history bigger than he: a battle of baseball giants as intense as any pitcher-batter confrontation ever could be.

Outside of his weight (he was an imposing 240 pounds at the time), the biggest problem Ruth had as the season began was money. Raised without money and lacking the self-discipline to manage it, he spent what he earned moments

The Babe and Home Run Baker would team up to make 1921 a very interesting year.

after it reached his hands. People paid him for endorsements, he had articles for newspapers ghost-written under his name, and he was always broke. Leaving $50 tips for ham sandwiches wasn't uncommon. He fell for a reported horse-racing scam in Cuba after the 1920 season (a terrible mistake in judgement that cost him $25,000), and he gambled away nearly all of his $40,000 earnings while on the trip. He invested money in a series of movies that never saw the light, or even the camera. Even worse, when he sued the Curtiss Candy Company because they had released a candy bar called "Baby Ruth," Curtiss claimed it had been named for the young daughter of former President Cleveland, not for him. "Baby Ruth" Cleveland had died 17 years earlier. Incredulously, the judge believed the company, and even worse, declared that Babe's own candy company could not market a bar called "Ruth's Home Run." *The Sporting News* ran an article tut-tutting Ruth's behavior, making reference to "giants with the brains of a boy."

Miller Huggins and Ping Bodie flank the Babe in the dugout at spring training in 1921.

Endorsements became big business for the Bambino.

Enter Christy Walsh, the businessman's Brother Matthias, the second person to save Babe Ruth from himself. A clever promoter who wanted to syndicate ghost-written sports columns under the names of famous athletes, Walsh found a ruse (delivering beer) to speak to Ruth, promised him a fortune if he would sign up, and guaranteed him a check for $1,000 before spring training. Ruth agreed. Walsh borrowed $1,000 for the up-front money, and a long and highly profitable relationship began. Ruth had received around $500 for his pre-Walsh ghostwriting efforts; in 1921 he would receive $15,000. With the Babe as his centerpiece, Walsh went on to build an empire of syndicated sports columns, "writ-

ten" by everyone from Knute Rockne to John McGraw. Even more importantly, Walsh became Ruth's financial adviser and put his money into safe investments, investments that would pay off for Ruth even during the Depression. Financially, it was exactly what the Babe needed.

Even though Ruth was able to sweat off 10 pounds in the baths of Hot Springs, more high times were the order of the day for the 1921 Yankees' spring training in Shreveport, Louisiana. A local car dealer let Babe have free use of a classy car during spring training. The auto had no license plate; its identification was the spare wheel cover brightly emblazoned "Babe Ruth's Essex." The Essex and its owner had great fun out and about in Shreveport. The rest of the Yankees seemed to be following his lead: long, raucous parties were followed by days of highly successful baseball. The Dodgers and Yankees traveled north together after spring training, playing 14 exhibitions en route. The Yanks emerged victorious nine times.

The Babe and Dodger Otto Miller shag a few at Hot Springs.

Several players acquired during the offseason improved the team. Frank "Home Run" Baker was cajoled out of retirement to become a Yank. Waite Hoyt, on his way to an excellent pitching career, and muscular catcher Wally Schang arrived in the same deal from the Red Sox, as the Yankees continued their pillaging of the once-glorious franchise. The Sox seemed hypnotized when they dealt with Colonels Ruppert and Huston.

Perhaps the most significant arrival from Boston was not a player but a suit named Ed Barrow. Barrow, who had been the Red Sox manager when the Ruth-led pitching staff won the Sox the 1918 World Series, was a gruff, tough baseball man with bushy eyebrows and a rugged countenance. The Yankees hired him because his eye for talent was keen; an early signer of Honus Wagner, he was instrumental in the many deals that would make the Yankees legends and the Red Sox impoverished.

He helped build the first Yankee farm system.

As the season started, Ruth was killing the ball. By the middle of June, he had belted 24 homers, including seven in a five-day stretch. In the first 18 days of July he slugged eight more. Keep in mind, these were not cheap shots; local writers gave him credit for hitting the "longest balls ever" in D.C., St. Louis, Detroit, and Shibe Park in Philadelphia. Much to his credit, Babe was demonstrating baseball smarts, too. When infielders played him too deep, he was not averse to a clever bunt for an infield single.

His antics were not confined to the field. Various legal spats caused him grief. He was sued for not paying automobile taxes for his newest car, a Stutz Bearcat. On June 8 he was pulled over for speeding in the Bearcat for the second time that year. The judge fined him $100 (which Babe paid by peeling off a single C-note from the wad of bills in his pocket), but the judge demanded he spend the day in jail; it was a second offense, after all. Forced to stew in a cell for several hours, Ruth sent for his game uniform and dressed there. When he left for the game, a thousand fans cheered him on, and newspaper and newsreel photographers recorded the event.

While his other excesses have become part of baseball lore, his wildest may have been his driving. The sight of Ruth speeding down

Opening Day, 1921. There was much ado about hot-hitting Ruth.

As the Babe slammed the sport into a new era, it meant the scientific "inside baseball" of Ty Cobb was on the endangered list.

Riverside Drive in the most expensive car he could buy was a common New York sight. He was as reckless behind the wheel as he was anywhere. He was always paying for cars he had rammed or for speeding tickets he had been charged with.

Ruth, Baker, and Meusel made short work of any pitcher they faced.

Huggins was unable to control his high-living players. Besides, even though the pitching staff was wearing thin, they kept winning, so they probably wouldn't have listened anyway. The Yankees clinched the pennant on October 1. Cleveland was second at 4½ games back. Ruth's batting numbers were beyond belief. His 59 homers bested his own previous mark by five and added up to 35 more homers than the number two man. He scored 45 more runs than the second-place finisher. With 44 doubles and 16 triples, he totalled 92 more bases than the batter who finished second. He batted in 171 runs, 32 more than the runnerup, and walked 144 times. Only one other player walked more than 100 times in that season. Babe's batting average was third behind Harry Heilman and Ty Cobb. His on-base percentage was 60 points higher than Cobb's. His slugging average was a stratospheric .846. (The year before it had been .847. Nobody other than Lou Gehrig has ever slugged above .757.)

The Bambino flags one down in right.

The 1921 World Series was rightly seen as a clash of baseball styles, with the hit-and-run "little ball" of John McGraw's Giants doing battle with the big belters of Ruth and Bob Meusel (who had hit 24 homers and knocked in 135 runs himself). In retrospect, we can see it as a clash of baseball eras, between the successful strategies made nec-

Despite heroic efforts from the Babe, the 1921 New York Yankees clinched the pennant but lost the World Series.

essary by the dead ball and the new wave of long-distance slugging encouraged by the livelier and cleaner sphere. At the time, no one could be sure which style would win out. The bookmakers put the Series at even money.

When Ruth's first at bat in Game 1 drove in the first run, McGraw shifted strategy, making certain Ruth wouldn't see many good pitches. The Yanks won Games 1 and 2. Ruth, frustrated after walking for the third time in Game 2, put his feet to work and stole second and third. On his slide into third, he scraped his arm near the elbow. The cut became infected.

In Game 3, he drove in two runs with a single in the Yankees loss, but he was obviously in pain. He had to be removed for a pinch runner in the eighth inning. The abscess that had formed on his arm had to be lanced. A rain out cancelled the next day's game, but Ruth returned to the lineup, injured arm and all, on October 9.

With only one good arm, he hit a home run, which led writer Heywood Hale Broun to coin one of the many great Ruthisms: "The Ruth is mighty and shall prevail." The Yanks, however, lost again.

Babe started Game 5, still in sad shape. A drainage tube led out of his arm, a sore wrist was heavily taped, as were his battered legs. Bloodied but unbowed, he slapped a surprise bunt single in the fourth inning and scored what proved to be the winning run all the way from first on Meusel's two-bagger. With Ruth still exhausted after his wild dash around the bases on a punch-drunk body, Huggins had to call time until the Babe could catch his breath and take his position in the outfield. When the crowd saw him leave the dugout, they went crazy.

Babe Ruth: His Life and Times

That night the doctors gave him a terrifying report. If he tried to play again, they said, he would certainly require another incision to drain the wound further. The result could be a permanent crippling. He was ordered not to play.

Then, just as there has been throughout time, there was a wise guy. Joe Vila, a prominent (and highly opinionated) sportswriter of the time wrote a blistering column in which he accused Babe of lying. He said Ruth tricked the fans "by going into the game after the report had been spread that he had been forced out of the Series by an operation on his 'infected elbow.'"

When Ruth arrived at the ballpark the next day, someone showed him Vila's

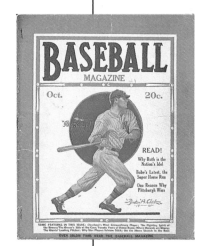

In this 1921 issue of Baseball Magazine, *the slugger's fame had earned him the title of "the Nation's idol."*

column. The enraged Bambino rushed to meet Vila in the press boxes, where he thrust the ugly, bandaged, and draining elbow in Vila's face and shouted, "Why don't you take a picture of this and put it in your paper?" Vila remained coy. His next day's column said, "Peeved over something that had appeared in print, Ruth tried to pick a fight with a newspaper writer. . . . Ruth, it seems, is no different from other baseball stars who consider praise and flattery belongs to them as a matter of course but are unable to stand criticism without showing their true colors." It may have been true that Ruth was sensitive to criticism, but he was certainly no faker. Baseball was what he did, and he never wanted to do anything more.

The Giants won the next three games (this was the last of the three-year best-of-nine World Series experiment) and won the Series. Ruth could manage only a ground out as a pinch hitter in the eighth game.

After several days of forced bench-sitting, Ruth's arm was healing rapidly. A seldom-noticed but unassailable fact is that the bodies of superior athletes repair themselves more quickly than those of the rest of us. It's part of the package. Babe, as one of the most incredible physical specimens of all time, was a rapid healer. Ruth had plans to take Bob Meusel and several other Yankees on a postseason barnstorming tour.

The word "barnstorming" arose from old vaudeville days when shows went on the road and were willing and eager to play anywhere, even in a barn. Baseball teams had done it since the 1860s. Albert G. Spalding led a world-wide barnstorming expedition in the 1870s. It was a great way to make extra money without hard work. Fans who couldn't normally see major league players loved the games, the players

had fun playing them, and all seemed to work out well. In fact, the first "World Series," in the 1880s, was just such postseason baseball tours.

However, by 1914 owners weren't so keen on the idea. First off, they didn't make any money on the deal; the players did. Second, the players might get hurt. Barnstorming also diminished the importance of their own official postseason championships, as the two pennant winners could sign up with local promoters to "replay the World Series" on tiny fields across the country. However, no one from Organized Baseball had stepped forward to enforce the rule stringently.

Enter Judge Kenesaw Mountain Landis. Landis, a federal judge without a genuine law degree (not uncommon at the time), was a braggadocio "enemy of the trusts," whose rulings were usually overturned by higher courts. The Judge, who loved baseball, heard the Federal League's suit against the majors and judiciously refused to make a ruling until the Feds collapsed under their own weight. His inaction earned Landis the undying gratitude of the major league owners. When the

Inquiring minds want to know! Columbia University ran tests on the Bambino to explore his hand, eye, and muscle coordination.

Babe Ruth: His Life and Times

Ever the showman, the Babe enjoyed the novel tests for distance that were presented him.

"Black Sox" scandal broke in 1920, mutually destructive strife among the owners kept them from taking forceful action. So they appointed Judge Landis to the post of commissioner and gave him supreme power to act in the best interest of the game.

Landis certainly looked the part, with the craggy, imperious visage and stern, morally inspired, withering stare. He took the owners at their word: He did whatever *he* felt was best for baseball. He tossed eight members of the suspected (but not convicted) White Sox out of the game forever. Other players who brought with them the slightest whiff of improper behavior were dismissed. Even owners felt his wrath; he ordered Charles Stoneham and John McGraw to sell off their gambling interests.

When Commissioner Landis heard that Ruth, Meusel, and a few others were planning to take their show on the road, he acted instantly, calling Ruth to command that he stay home. Ruth, not surprisingly, refused. He was on his way to catch the train that would take him to Buffalo, first stop in the tour.

"Oh, you are, are you? That's just fine. But if you do, it will be the sorriest thing you ever did in baseball," the enraged judge shouted before he slammed down the receiver. He proceeded to rail at length at the young Ruth's boldness in gutter language. Landis saw the World Series as his domain, and he desperately needed to establish the legitimacy of that Series as a championship, not just another exhibition. Anyone trying to challenge that was defying him personally.

Ruth wasn't intimidated. What could Landis do—refuse to pay him his World Series share? The fact is, playing the World Series *cost* Babe Ruth money. A good barnstorming tour could put $25,000 in his pocket. Landis laid down the law in frighteningly direct terms: "This case resolves itself into a question of who is the biggest man in baseball, the Commissioner or the player who makes the most home runs." Ruth's bosses, Huston and Ruppert, quietly concurred with the Chief.

The tour didn't make much money. Bad weather rained out many games. Other cities feared Landis's wrath and cancelled. Many minor league teams, also cowed by the Commissioner, forbade the barnstormers to use their fields.

The barnstorming over, Ruth went on a vaudeville tour with performer Wellington Cross. The biggest laugh of their act came when a "messenger" delivered a "telegram." Ruth said his line, "It's from Judge Landis."

Cross would then respond, "Is it serious?" "I'll say," Ruth replied. "Seventy-five cents, collect."

Landis waited until December to hand down his rulings. He withheld World Series shares from Ruth and Meusel and then suspended them from playing until May 20, 1922. It would cost them each 39 days without pay. Ruth was advised to beg for leniency. He went quail hunting instead.

In his spare time, Ruth often hit the links. His trademark follow-through was ever present.

Though an athlete of rare proportions, the 26-year-old Ruth was still an adolescent emotionally. He was good-hearted—with his first 1922 paycheck he bought a Cadillac for St. Mary's—but confused.

Imagine the poor Babe's emotional muddle. Here he was, a supremely gifted athlete playing the game he loved most dearly at a level of profound excellence no one had ever seen before. His awesome physical skills were at their peak. He was making money no ballplayer had ever approached, more money in one season than most Americans would see in 10 years of work. Early in 1922, he signed a three-year contract for $52,000 a year, more than three times as much as the next highest-paid Yankee. (The story goes, the extra $2,000 were determined by a coin flip because Babe "liked the idea" of making a thousand dollars a week.) He was earning that much again in outside deals, endorsements, vaudeville, and barnstorming. Yet here he was, banned from playing baseball. Banned from doing what he did best (not to mention *better* than anyone else), and banned from making money at it. The reason?

He had played baseball and made money at it.

Interestingly, the ban of Ruth and Meusel did not apply during spring training. Ruth had singlehandedly turned the expected dollar losses of southern spring work-outs into positive cash flow for the team. People paid to see the big lug, no matter where it was. So the team made money. Some say the Yankees made enough on spring training ticket sales to pay Ruth's salary for the entire season. The imperious Landis had no qualms about penalizing the boy-man and his cohort for disobedience, but he could not see fit to take money out of the ample pockets of Ruppert and Huston.

Babe and Bob Meusel pleaded their case with Judge Landis (center). Their protestations failed.

During the spring, Landis made a trip to New Orleans (a curious place to locate spring training for a high-living bunch like the Yankees). There, Ruth and Meusel met with him to plead their case for early reinstatement. Landis had already received a petition signed by 10,000 New Yorkers begging for just that. When the two players left, apparently having heard both barrels of a full-blown Landis diatribe, only Babe could speak. His comment: "That guy sure can talk." That night Lan-

dis attended a charity game and auction. He proceded to outbid everyone ($250) to win a Ruth-autographed baseball.

Landis wanted more than contrition. He wanted a promise that Ruth would never go on off-season barnstorming tours again. Unless, of course, they were tours from spring training north, in which the Yankees would make most of the money. Ruth bristled against that idea until Huston asked him, "What would happen to the Yankees if you and Meusel got suspended for a whole year?" The Babe saw the light. He was also named captain, a largely honorary title, but one that meant much to him.

The Yankees, bolstered by the addition of durable infielder Everett Scott, pitchers Joe Bush and Sad Sam Jones from the Red Sox (who else?), and outfielder Whitey Witt from the Athletics, were looking forward to another pennant-winning season. The season began, despite pleadings to Landis from around the country, without Ruth and Meusel out with the team before the games, then retire to a box seat or go home. During the layoff, the bored Ruth and Meusel had their tonsils out. (At the time it was considered a preventive action.)

Before one game Ruth showed up with a little girl, about two years old, and introduced her as his daughter, Dorothy. While it did not become clear until years later, Dorothy was adopted. This fact mattered not one bit to the huge kid. It was obvious he loved her.

While the Yankees managed to win 22 games (and lose 11) before the return of their two hitting stars, estimates indicate that the Yanks saw $100,000 less in gross receipts without the Babe as a draw.

Together again. Owner Jake Ruppert was all smiles when Ruth and Meusel could suit up for action again.

A rosy-cheeked Ruth graces another cover.

The big guy's pretzel-like finish to his mammoth swing was a crowd pleaser.

Ruth and Meusel were reinstated by Landis in time for the game on Saturday, May 20. Ruth, delighted to be in uniform, couldn't have known he was on the way to one of his worst seasons ever—in every respect.

Ruth's first game back was a disaster. He struck out, twice popped out, and also grounded out. The crowd turned on him. They began to boo. The fans did not seem to want to forgive their hero. The booing increased as the games continued, and Ruth failed to hit. The Polo Grounds faithful began to deliver nasty applause when he caught easy fly balls. Babe responded in turn by sarcastically tipping his cap to the throng.

In only his fifth game back, the pressure got to him. After being thrown out trying to stretch a single into a double, Ruth threw a handful of dirt in umpire George Hildebrand's face. Hildebrand tossed him from the game, and as Ruth neared the Yankees dugout a fan in the stands screamed something nasty at him. Babe charged into the stands after the heckler, who scampered away.

League President Ban Johnson announced a suspension pending an investigation. Ruth, who had hardly ever missed a game, regular season or exhibition, in years, had been ejected for the first time ever and suspended for the second time in one year.

Once again, money talked. The Yanks' next game was scheduled for Washington, where tight-fisted owner Clark Griffith earned big checks on the days Babe Ruth played. Griffith needed the money. Johnson reinstated Babe after one day, ordered a $200 fine, and took away his title of captain. His "promotion" had lasted just six days.

Even though the Yankees were winning, managing to stay close to the St. Louis Browns in the standings, they were causing havoc with Manager Huggins's ulcers. Huggins sent a private detective to follow them on road trips, posing as a rich "sport." There were fights in the dugout between players and between Huggins and players. Landis made a special trip to address the team in the clubhouse about their behavior. It didn't help.

Spats with the men in blue continued, too. In the middle of June, Ruth came charging in from left field to argue a call at second base by umpire Bill Dineen. What he said led to a three-day suspension. The next day before the game Ruth challenged Dineen to a fight under the stands, which was avoided, but Johnson tacked two more days onto Ruth's suspension. Ejected for disputing a called third strike late in August, Ruth was suspended three more days, making a total of five suspensions (if you count both the preseason one and the addition to the first Dineen suspension).

Little Dorothy Ruth tries to emulate her famous daddy.

There was another reason that 1922 was a bad season for Ruth. It was the first time he had to face lefty Hub Pruett of the St. Louis Browns. Pruett had a sneaky little screwball that broke the opposite direction of a regular curve. The first 14 times Babe faced the youngster, he struck out 10 times and walked twice. The only time he managed to put his bat on the ball, he just rolled it right back to the pitcher. In a critical game in September, Ruth seemed to remove the curse when he homered and singled in consecutive appearances against Hub.

Pruett never pitched in the American League after 1924 (which certainly

At his Home Plate Farm, we see a domesticated side of the Bambino.

pleased Ruth), and although Ruth's average against the lefty improved over the next few years, Pruett's mastery of the Babe became a legend. Another pitcher, righthander George Uhle, was also tough on the Babe. However, unlike Pruett, he was tough on everybody. Uhle was an early master of the slider. Those who want to claim that Babe Ruth's batting numbers would have been lower if he had to face screwball and slider pitchers more often (as those pitches boomed in popularity later) may have a case when one looks at Ruth's performances versus Pruett and Uhle.

To raise money for the Widows' Pension Fund for the NYC PD, Bob Meusel stood on top of a building on Broadway (175 feet up), throwing baseballs to the waiting Babe below.

Aided by another former Boston player, "Jumpin' Joe" Dugan, in July, the Yankees held on to win the pennant by one game. Despite playing only 110 games, Ruth led the league in slugging percentage and batted .315 (league leader George Sisler batted 105 points higher). It was the first time in five years—since he became a regular, in fact—that he failed to lead the league in home runs, finishing third with 35. Only once over the course of the next 10 years would he fail to lead the league.

If Ruth thought it was his worst season, many would have to agree. The suspensions, the fines, the booing, and his efforts in the World Series all took their toll. Facing the Giants again, Ruth was stymied when McGraw ordered his pitchers to throw nothing but curves "low on the outside" to the Babe. He struggled to hit just one single and one double in 17 at bats, driving in only one run as the Giants swept the Yanks in four games.

During the Series, the crowds and the other players were tough on the Babe. Notably, there was some particularly venomous name-calling from the Giants bench.

The Babe contemplates some weighty issues.

Babe could usually take the foul-languaged banter that came at him from opponents, and he could dish it out, too, but he found these personal attacks to be too much. After one of the games he charged into the Giant clubhouse to challenge a player who had been particularily abusive. Luckily the tempers were cooled before any fighting occurred.

It was about this time that Colonel Huston disagreed with one of Huggins's managerial decisions and served notice that the tiny manager's days with the Yankees were numbered. Colonel Ruppert overruled Huston, but the rift between the two was insoluble. The next May, Huston sold his share in the team back to Ruppert for $1.5 million, six times what he had paid for it in 1915.

Surprisingly, Ruth took off after the Series for another barnstorming tour. Landis, having made his point, saw to it that the owners changed the rule. In retrospect, it's hard to believe that people in Iowa and North Dakota would confuse a fun-loving visit to their town by a bunch of ballplayers with the World Series. Landis's rigorous action against Ruth, however, served to solidify his control of the game.

Ruth returned to New York and Christy Walsh, acting as a good businessman, suggested that Babe make a gesture to let the fans know he was mending his ways. Walsh organized a dinner honoring Ruth at the New York Elks Club. This fete featured a "Back to the Farm" theme (including a papier-mâchè cow) and a freewheeling question-and-answer session with the Babe.

Unfortunately, an up-and-coming politico by the name of Jimmy Walker (soon to be New York's mayor, and no saint himself) took this opportunity to give a passionate speech. It was during this speech that he let Babe have it with both barrels: for his cavorting, late-night escapades, and huge appetite that kept him constantly out of shape. After scolding Ruth noisily, he played his trump card. He asked Ruth, "Are you going to keep letting down those dirty-faced little kids?"

Ruth was deeply touched. Some claimed he wept. He vowed to go to his Sudbury farm with Helen and Dorothy, work hard, and swear off drink.

He did just that. Ruth, now 27 years old, was able to whip his tired body into first-rate condition. He reported to training camp weighing a healthy 215, far from overweight for his 6'2" frame. The flu bug that seemed to nab him every spring reappeared, and Babe dropped 13 more pounds before the team headed north, to one of his greatest triumphs—the opening of Yankee Stadium.

The Babe and his bovine friend at the Christy Walsh-inspired event.

After the 1920 season, the ownership of the Giants, always fretful about the "other" New York team's success, informed the Yankees that they would no longer be welcome at the Polo Grounds. Yankee management offered to buy a half-interest in the park, raze it, and build an "all-sports pleasure palace" that would seat as many as 100,000 fans. Giants boss Charles Stoneham refused the offer. The Yankees bought a site across the Harlem River from the Giants' park for $600,000 and began building Yankee Stadium in early '22. Although the price of $2.5 million was rather steep, Yankee management was proud of their glorious new edifice. It was the first new park to open in the majors in nine years. (There had been 10 between 1909 and 1914, as baseball's popularity boomed and the new technology of structural steel came into the picture.)

Opening Day, April 17, 1923, was a spectacular day for everyone, even if the weather was cloudy and cool. The Yankees beat the hapless Red Sox 4-1. True to his legend, Ruth hit a three-run homer, the first ever in the new park. This prompted Fred Lieb to promptly dub the stadium, "The House that Ruth Built." Yankee general manager Barrow proudly announced the attendance at a spectacular 74,217. Estimates say 25,000 people were turned away. However, a month later it was discovered that the Stadium seated only 62,000. There had not been 12,000 standing room tickets sold for the opener. The official Yankee response: "It was an estimate."

After working hard on the farm, Ruth sees the results of his efforts.

Two people came into Babe Ruth's life in 1923 who would become major influences on his life and career. That year the Yankees signed a big strong kid from the campus of Columbia University, Lou Gehrig. Gehrig became the quiet counterpart to Ruthian excess, yet nearly his match as a batter. The duo's batting feats are almost impossible to comprehend. (Gehrig wouldn't join the Yanks full time until 1925.)

The other person was Claire Hodgson. Unlike the nervous, somewhat plain-looking Helen Ruth, Claire was poised, self-confident, and very attractive. She had left a bad marriage in Georgia in 1920, traveled to New York with her daughter, Julia, and started a career. Her elegant good looks soon got her work as a model for well-known illustrators. Her husband died two years later.

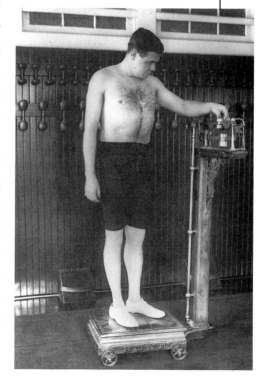

She began an acting career, and while working in a play opening in Washington, a friend in the cast asked her to join him to see the Yankees play the Senators. Claire was a baseball fan. She had met Ty Cobb through her connections in modeling and the theater. His friend also knew Babe Ruth. They met briefly before the game. Although he didn't act it at the time, the Babe was smitten.

Actress Claire Hodgson had caught the slugger's eye.

He sent an invitation to the theater that night asking her to join him for dinner. Her return note asked if she could bring along a lady friend; Ruth's reputation had preceded him. A phone call ensued in which the Babe agreed to terms but said they'd have to have dinner in his hotel suite, because if he went to a restaurant, they'd be mobbed. He always was. "Don't worry, though," he added. "The place will be full of people. It always is."

This spread on the Yankees and Tigers ran in the 1923 New York Times.

By the time the show opened in New York, Claire had been joined by her mother and two brothers (their father had died earlier that year). Ruth began to spend much of his free time in their company, entertaining her mom and charming Claire. Babe and Helen lived quite separate lives now. Helen and Dorothy stayed on the Sudbury farm throughout 1923, except for their spring training trip and one visit by Helen to the city. It seemed best for the child to be away from the raucous circus atmosphere that surrounded her adoptive father. Living in the city, Babe found himself wrapped up in the courting of this new woman in his life. Claire was different than Helen. She was someone who could live in the bright lights when necessary and help rein him in when required. Divorce from Helen was out of the question; Ruth had been raised a Catholic.

On the field the Yankees were dominating. With the preseason arrival of pitchers Herb Pennock and George Pipgras from the Red Sox, the Yankee starting eight featured four former Boston players, and six of their eight pitchers were originally Boston property as well. Harry Frazee, having completed the devastation, sold the Red Sox that August.

The Yankees led the American League from Opening Day. After the middle of June, no club was within five games of them. They finished 16 lengths ahead of second-place Detroit. The Red Sox were 37 games back, seven games out of seventh place. Attendance around the American League was down. Fans became bored with how easily the Yankees quashed the opposition.

As a batter, Ruth was merely sensational. He led the AL in seven categories, including on-base percentage and slugging average. He walloped a dozen more homers than the runner-up. His batting average was .393, the highest mark of his career and second only to Harry Heilman's .403. The strategy of taking the bat from his hands didn't work; with all that offensive firepower, he still walked 170 times. No batter has ever walked more in one season. The next closest man received 72 fewer free passes. Ruth won the Most Valuable Player Award hands down. There is debate about which of Ruth's seasons was the most impressive overall, but Ruth told a biographer that to him 1923 was his "peak year."

The World Series pitted John McGraw's Giants against Ruth and the Yankees once again. McGraw took the un-

For the Babe, 1923 was a banner year. His superior efforts on the field made for a sensational season. Still, he always made time to bring a smile to those who needed one most.

usual step, for the time, of calling all the pitches his hurlers threw to Ruth. He explained it by saying, "Ballplayers can do a more workmanlike job when they feel someone else is taking the responsibility." The Yankees lost Game 1 by one run (5-4) when Casey Stengel hit an inside-the-park home run in the top of the ninth inning. As Stengel was rounding first, a pad in his shoe meant to protect a sore heel slipped loose. Stengel thought his shoe was coming off, so his usual speedy step was thrown askew. The description of his gait by Damon Runyon in the next day's newspaper has become a baseball classic.

What kid wouldn't want one of these?

Counting this defeat in Game 1, the Yankees had lost eight consecutive Series games to the Giants: the last three in 1921 when Ruth was out with the abscessed elbow followed by the 1922 four-game sweep. Things were about to change.

In Game 2 of the 1923 Series, Ruth belted two homers. The first blast went over the Polo Grounds rightfield roof, and the second helped the Yankees to a 4-2 victory.

Stengel won Game 3 (1-0). Again a home run provided the punch, this one heading over the fence. When he thumbed his nose at the Yankees bench as he rounded third, the Yanks pretended to be aghast. They asked Landis to take action. The Commissioner commented, "When a guy hits two home runs to win two World Series games, he deserves a little fun." Stengel, as fate would have it, provided the only excitement for Giants fans in the Series. The Yanks exploded for six runs in the second inning of Game 4, scored seven in the first two frames of Game 5, and blew open a tight match in Game 6 with five runs in the eighth.

The Yankees were world champions for the first time. In his 19 times at bat, Ruth hit three homers and scored eight runs. McGraw's pitch-calling walked him eight times. With an overall attendance of 302,000 for the six games, gross receipts reached $1 million. The Yankees each took home $6,160.46 for their win; the Giants $4,112.81. That record stood until 1935.

The Babe still loved being with kids. Lots of them. During his annual post-season barnstorming tour, 6,000 kids swarmed onto the field after one game, flattening the superstar. They continued piling on their hero until four police officers were able to clear them off. The laughing Babe arose uninjured and wanted to throw baseballs to them, but the cops, fearing a riot, refused.

During spring training of 1924, Jocko Conlan (later to earn fame as a major league umpire) was a player with the Rochester Red Wings, in the middle of an exhibition series with the Yankees. Conlan tells this story:

"At Mobile there was a large crowd. After the game the teams went to their hotel and had dinner and Ruth still hadn't come back [from the game]. He finally came in about eight o'clock without his cap; his shirt was torn, his fielding glove was tied to his belt with a cord, and his baseball suit was all muddy with Alabama clay up above his knees. The reporters asked Ruth, 'Where were you?' Ruth said, 'There were about 75 kids who stayed in the park and wanted to play ball. I spent all the time since the game hitting flies and shagging flies with the kids.'"

While he might have been called out on this play in the fifth of Game 1, the Babe would not be down for long.

This now-familiar scene occurred wherever the big kid went.

As had become his custom, Ruth reported to Hot Springs to sweat and golf off the extra pounds the winter had added to his frame. He was about 240 when the recurrent spring flu got him again. Burning with fever, he sweated off 22 pounds in a few weeks. The biggest news Babe made during spring training that year was losing a $1,000 bill somewhere between the team's hotel and the bank. He had four of them to start with.

The 1924 season was dismal for the Yankees. The team was aging; four regulars and nearly all their bench were over 30. That didn't keep them away from the speakeasies and parties; they were as boisterous a bunch of noisemakers as ever. Their performances, however, slipped drastically.

Except for the Babe.

He may have been leading the party brigade, but at age 29, he had plenty of life in him to burn the candle at both ends. In fact, 1924 is the first year that Ruth biographers mention his frequent use of bicarbonate of soda to quell the rumblings of an overfed stomach. For Babe, the bubbly drink was just what the doctor ordered. He'd revel throughout the night, then before each game, down a few hot dogs and several bottles of soda pop, drink some bicarb, emit a Ruthian belch, and go merrily on his way.

The players' tempers weren't calmed by their escapades off the field. Ruth was at the center of an on-field brawl with Ty Cobb. The fray led to several ejections and fines, and the forfeiture of the game to the Yankees when angry Detroit fans stormed the field. The team was out

Although his body had already taken years of punishment, the Babe didn't let it stop him from hook sliding like a pro.

The Babe spends some time with daughter Dorothy in 1924.

The 1924 Yankees. This photo was the first taken of the team since Miller Huggins had taken over as manager.

of control, and nothing Manager Huggins could do seemed to make any difference. He shipped off one of his more surly (though highly talented) pitchers, Carl Mays, to Cincinnati in midseason, and the Yanks never recovered. After starting the season hot, the Yankees fell behind the surging Washington Senators. Without Mays, the Yanks were unable to catch up and finished two games back. The Senators' late charge, winning 16 of their final 21, made the difference.

Ruth kept his sense of humor. Perhaps nothing would top the event that happened just the summer before. It was a very hot day, and the team was to meet President Harding before a game. When it was Babe's turn to shake his hand, he stopped, wiped his huge brow with a huge handkerchief, and said, "Hot as hell, ain't it, Prez?"

Ruth finished the season by winning his first and only batting title. He won the home run title again and led the league in runs, total bases, walks, on-base percentage, and slugging average. Goose Goslin of the Senators wound up driving in 129 runs to Babe's 121, and Babe didn't win the Triple Crown. (He never would.)

The Babe's most successful barnstorming tour ever took place that fall. His and Meusel's teams traveled 8,500 miles and played in 15 cities before 125,000 people. Out of 15 games, Babe's team won every one; he also hit 17 homers.

According to biographer Smelser, in 1924 Babe Ruth's signature appeared on 10,000 balls and 2,000 bats. He had taught the Yankee trainer how to forge his signature.

Ruth spent the postseason of 1924 in usual form: overeating, overpartying. His marriage to Helen was on the rocks. Frail, sensitive, and naive to begin with, she was less and less able to cope with the well-publicized gargantuan habits of her husband.

When the Yanks obtained pitcher Urban Shocker from St. Louis, Huggins confidently announced that the 1925 Yankees were the strongest team he had ever managed. He couldn't have been more wrong. The team was old. Young Lou Gehrig would begin his career as a Yank that year, Earle Combs was a flashy centerfielder, and Bob Meusel could still hit, but there was little else to admire. Worst of all, they had to begin the season without Babe Ruth.

Ruth had signed a two-year contract extension for the same $52,000 per year of his old contract. He headed for Hot Springs to sweat off the 40 or so extra pounds he was carrying, but it didn't work. In March, a pitch broke the tip of one of Ruth's fingers.

When he reached the training camp in St. Petersburg, Florida, he looked awful, and Huggins told him so. Babe replied, inimitably, "I've got a temperature of a hundred and five and eight fifths." The annual battle with flu seemed to be back, only much worse this time. He was still out of shape when the team began its northward exhibition swing against the Dodgers. After a game in Atlanta, Ruth saw a doctor, who advised against his continuing with the team. His fever really hadn't subsided much, and he was weak. Typically, Ruth ignored the advice and played the next day in Chattanooga. Despite the cold, rainy weather, and his still-frail condition, he slugged two home runs. They said one of them traveled more than 400 feet. At the time he was hitting .449, even though he had lost 21 pounds because of the illness.

The next leg of the rail trip was to Asheville, North Carolina, a winding, difficult tour through the Smoky Mountains. Ruth wasn't the only one who was feeling poorly. Several other players were nauseated by the

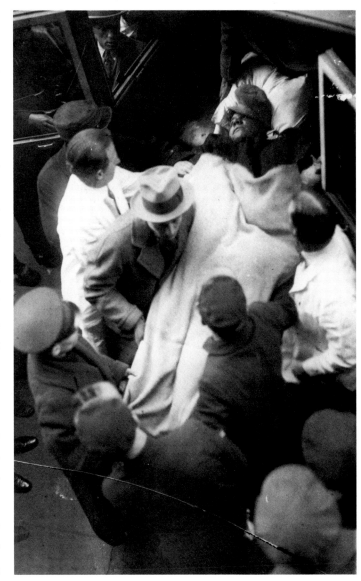

A terrifying scene is captured on film. The "bellyache" that struck down the mighty Babe in 1925 made for some exaggerated news copy.

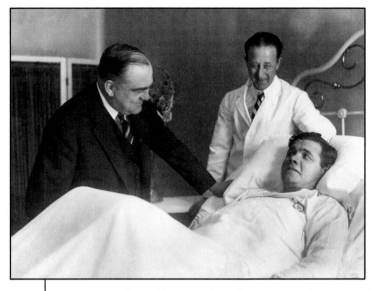

Ed Barrow and a doctor check on the ailing Babe's condition. After recuperating a bit, the Bambino was wheeled to the roof to catch some rays.

twists and turns of the track. When the relieved players disembarked to the solid platform in Asheville, Ruth collapsed. Catcher Steve O'Neill caught the slugger before his head cracked against the marble floor.

Newspapers in the United States reported that the Babe had a case of the "grip," then a common term for influenza. The *London Evening News*, however, reported his death and presented an obituary which mentioned, among other things, that because of his portliness Ruth chose to wear braces (suspenders) rather than a belt, and "this started the fashion for braces in the U.S."

Babe was sent to New York in the care of Yankee scout Paul Krichell. When their train was late making a connection in Washington, Canadian papers also announced that Ruth had died. Ruth's illness, at first nothing special to sports reporters (he got the flu every spring), soon made front page headlines. The Babe had done it again, they claimed: He had overindulged on pop and hot dogs, and all the bicarb in the world couldn't put him back together. It was dubbed "The Bellyache Heard 'Round the World."

On the train from D.C., Ruth was able to force down a large breakfast, the first decent meal the usually voracious hero had been able to stomach for days. It was too much for his sore gut, however, and he collapsed, vomiting. When

he came to, he collapsed again, in the men's room, and hurt his head on the wash-basin as he fell.

It was a distressing scene when Ruth and Krichell arrived at Penn Station in New York. One biographer estimates there may have been as many as 25,000 people waiting for them. The stretcher they brought was too large to turn around in-side the train, so they had to cut out the side of the train between two windows and make a huge hole to carry the Babe out that way. He had three more frightening convulsive attacks while on the stretcher. It took six men to hold him down. He met his wife there and could only manage to say, "Helen, I feel rotten," before they loaded him into the ambulance. Three times more during the ride to St. Vincent's Hospital the Babe's large body was thrown into convulsions.

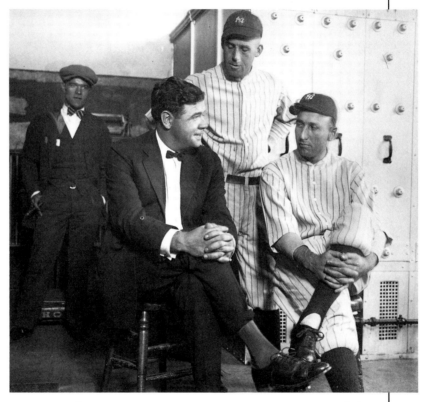

The convalescing slugger (shown here with Sam Jones and Ben Bengough) visited with his fellow pinstripers when possible.

At the hospital, the doc-tors were sanguine about his situation, claiming it was not serious, just a case of the flu, and that all he needed was rest. However, the next day they performed surgery for what was described as an "intestinal abscess," a brief but highly painful operation requiring two deep incisions. After such a medical procedure, Ruth couldn't return to the Yankees for seven weeks.

Speculation of all kinds has arisen as to what the "true" nature of Ruth's illness was. Of course the familiar children's story that he overdosed on hot dogs is absurd. Whatever it was, the nature of the illness was embarrassing enough that all the news-

A tearful Babe watched Helen's decline.

papermen in the country couldn't get any further clarification than "intestinal abscess." The Big Guy had had a Big Sickness.

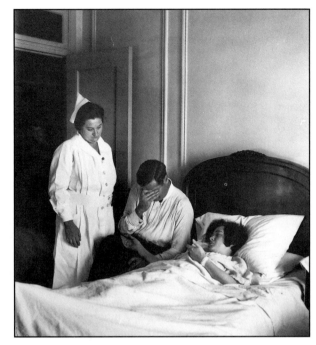

Ruth's remarkable recuperative powers demonstrated themselves soon after the operation, but the situation with his wife was worsening. Helen joined Babe in the hospital, and two weeks after his operation checked herself in. She had what was described as a nervous breakdown. There are photos showing Ruth sitting at her side, holding his teary face in his hands as he watched her deterioration. It was the final chapter in their relationship. For all intents and purposes, their marriage was over.

The day of Ruth's return was memorable for several reasons.

Babe left the hospital late in May and spent several days at the ballpark readying himself before he made his reappearance on June 1. By then the Yankees were already 10 games below .500, lost in seventh place. The day he made his re-entry into the lineup, however, is a day that will live in baseball history for another reason.

Everett Scott, the long-time shortstop, had played himself out of the lineup at age 32, ending his string of 1,307 consecutive games played, a record which pundits of the day (as they always do) predicted would never be broken. Scott's replacement was the hardly memorable Pee Wee Wanninger. The day Ruth returned, Lou Gehrig pinch-hit for Wanninger and began his streak of 2,130 consecutive games.

The team's overall poor play and the lack of the league's number one drawing card, however, cost AL clubs "at least" $200,000 in gate revenues. With his new lease on life, Ruth joined his fellow Yankees in creating new postgame highlights. The two-ended candle was burning brightly; Ruth complained about his health. "I might as well be 550 years old," he said late in June. The next day Huggins slapped a $1,000 fine on him for unspecified reasons. (Perhaps the fine had something to do with ongoing curfew violations.) However, when the Babe swatted two homers the next game, Huggins rescinded the fine.

The big guy is back and ready for action.

Ruth's health must have caused concern for Huggins. Ruth began to suffer from a series of bothersome, if minor, ailments, including an ankle he injured twice in the space of a week. On August 9, Bobby Veach pinch-hit for Ruth, a first since the Babe had left the pitching mound. By August 1, no less an authority than Fred Lieb felt

that "it is doubtful that Ruth will again be the superstar he was from 1919 through 1924." Lieb's logic sounded solid: Ruth was said to be 31 years old (he was actually 30; both he and the people of the time thought he was a year older; Babe had remembered his birth date incorrectly), but his body had much more wear and tear on it than Eddie Collins and Ty Cobb had at the same age, and they went downhill after that point.

The Huggins-Ruth relationship was always stormy. The Babe loved ragging the diminutive

A Monster of the Midway meets the Sultan of Swat. Chicago Bears running back Harold "Red" Grange poses with Ruth in 1925.

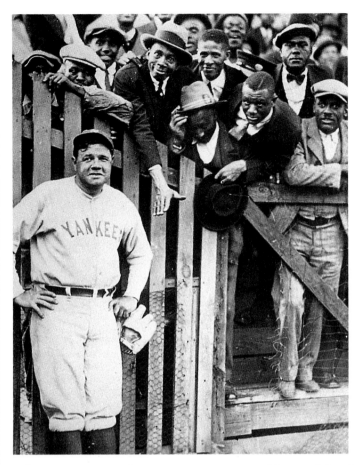

Every fan was important to the Babe. He was never too busy to pose for a picture or lend some baseball advice.

Huggins at every occasion. Babe's favorite nickname for his manager was the hardly complimentary "Little Boy." The tale is told that Ruth once grabbed the manager by the heels and hung him upside down off the back of a moving train, but that smacks a bit of sportswriter mythmaking. However, the situation between the two men came to a sour head late in August.

It seems that Ruth had spent three consecutive nights in St. Louis away from the team's hotel. When Huggins's private eye reported that the Babe had been holding court in a St. Louis bawdy house, the manager could take no more. The team was in trouble, and his leading star (currently batting just .245) was ignoring every rule in the book.

After getting approval from both Ruppert and Barrow, Huggins confronted Babe as he entered the clubhouse on August 29. "Don't bother getting dressed," the man-

ager informed him. "You've been fined $5,000 and suspended indefinitely." In huge disbelief, Ruth spun out of control. He threatened the small man physically and chewed him out in salty language.

The fine, an unheard-of amount, took everyone by surprise. Nobody

could remember anyone being fined more than $500 before. At nearly 10 percent of Ruth's salary, today's equivalent would be fining Barry Bonds for half a million dollars. Although Ruppert and Ruth remained friendly during the suspension (they even attended a few games together), Ruppert stood behind his manager.

Ruth sought the highest court of appeal he could think of: Judge Landis. Landis, however, was unavailable.

After a few days, the contrite Babe cooled off, and apologized, and apologized again. Huggins remained adamant throughout all the Babe's efforts. "I've heard that before," the manager said. It was not until nine days after the suspension that Huggins granted permission for the Babe to suit up and play again, on September 7. In retrospect, Ruth admitted he had overstepped the mark. "I was a babe and a boob."

The great Ruth had stumbled

Happy to be back in uniform and the bellyache behind him, the Babe had a tough row to hoe for a comeback. In true Ruthian style, however, he would not disappoint.

as only a man of his immense proportions could—hugely. He would, however, come back. Those prognosticators who doubted or predicted otherwise were in for a surprise. The "experts" were wrong about Babe Ruth again; he would come back greater than ever.

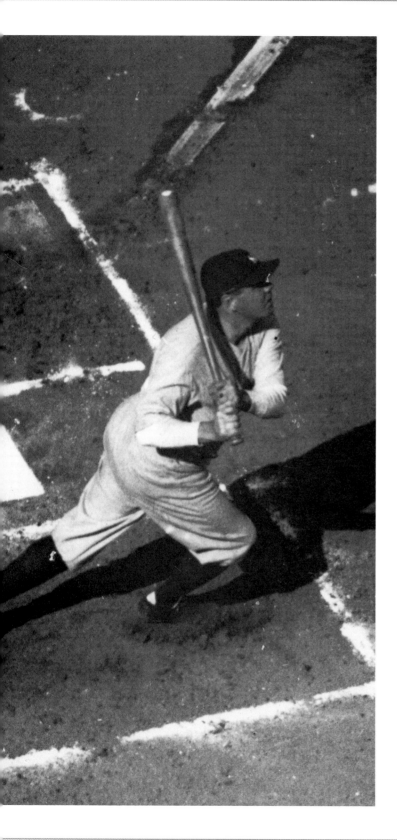

1926-1932

Tragedy and Triumph:
The Comeback "Keed"

"We've seen history made here today, a performance which will probably never be duplicated."

—Anonymous press box quote after the Babe hit three home runs in one game during the 1926 World Series

TRAGEDY AND TRIUMPH: THE COMEBACK "KEED"

Previous page: After a disappointing season in 1925, the Babe was out to prove he was truly the Sultan of Swat

After the 1925 season, it was hard to find a sportswriter—or anyone, for that matter—who didn't view the career of Babe Ruth as over. He was 31 years old, and an "old 31," as sports columnist Fred Lieb had said. He had already set a barrel full of batting records, with 356 career home runs, over 1,000 career RBI, and a batting average of .345. If the experts of the time had been right in their assessment that he was through, Ruth would still merit a spot on many all-time teams.

They were dead wrong. No one of his time really seemed to understand Ruth. They had overestimated his maturity in his earlier years, and they underestimated it in 1926. Ruth was still growing up, becoming the man that Brother Matthias saw in him 25 years before.

Ruth decided he needed to get in shape. He put himself under the punishing care of Manhattan gym owner Artie McGovern. McGovern was a stern taskmaster. Upon his arrival, Babe weighed in, tipping the scales at a portly 256 pounds. By the time he left for spring training, he was a slender and powerful 212. With four-hour workouts every day and strict supervision of Ruth's diet, McGovern had the Babe looking and feeling like the "keed" who had torn baseball apart in 1920 and 1921. Ruth's blood pressure improved; he lost nine inches off his waistline

After working out at McGovern's gym, Babe gets a once-over before reporting to spring training.

and six off his hips. By mid-January he had to order a whole new shirt wardrobe; the collars on his old ones were too large.

The 1926 Yankees were a team of potential but with a host of question marks. They had two rookies at the vital keystone positions: Mark Koenig and Tony Lazzeri. Lazzeri was already a bit of a legend himself. At that time, he was the only person in professional baseball history who had hit more home runs in a season than Babe Ruth. In 1925, over the course of 197 games in the Pacific Coast League, Tony had belted 60 homers. As a rookie, Lou Gehrig had established himself at first, but his .295 batting average and 20 home runs were hardly legend material (not yet, anyway). The pitching staff was downright old. Waite Hoyt, at 26, was the youngest starter (the next in line was six years his senior).

When the Yankees lost their first two spring training games to the Braves by a total of 28 runs, the "experts" jumped on the bandwagon. They were still wearing egg on their faces for predicting the 1925 team would finish first before it finished seventh. Writer Westbrook Pegler trumpeted that the '26 Yankees were "the worst team he ever saw" and were "sure to finish in last place."

What these prognosticators did not know was that the team was beginning to jell. The pitching was surprisingly effective and was bolstered by what would become one of the great offensive units of all time. The Yanks ended spring training with an 18-game winning streak, the last dozen being played against the Dodgers as the two teams traveled north together.

Part of the Babe's winter workout included indoor golf practice. He believed it drastically improved coordination. This photo from January 1926 illustrates his intense concentration.

143

Babe Ruth: His Life and Times

You can bet that every kid in New York was envious of this little guy.

Instead of holding their predicted last-place berth, the 1926 Yankees were never even in second place. A 16-game winning streak stretched their lead to six games and growing by June 1. On September 25, Ruth, Gehrig, and Meusel homered in succession. The trio's accomplishment marked the first time that had happened in the majors in 23 years. The Cleveland Indians, led by ace hurler and Ruth nemesis George Uhle, charged in August and September while the Yanks cooled off, allowing the Tribe to finish only three games back.

The Yankees' team ERA was only fourth in the league, but they outscored every other team by at least 45 runs. The spry young Gehrig led the league with 20 triples and added 16 homers to go with his .313 batting average. Lazzeri pitched in with 14 triples and 18 homers, and Meusel, despite breaking a bone in his foot and playing just 108 games, swatted a dozen homers and drove in 81. As a team, the Yanks were second in batting average but easily led the AL in on-base percentage and slugging average.

Ruth, meanwhile, had the kind of season everyone had predicted he never would again, leading the league in homers with 47, runs scored, RBI, and walks, and finishing second in batting average. To demonstrate that he was a team player, he laid down 10 sacrifice bunts, too. The sweat in McGovern's gym had paid off.

A figure from Ruth's past helped, too. In June, Chicago was the site of the International Eucharistic Congress, a huge gathering of devout Catholics.

The Yankees were in town at the same time, and they wisely invited Brother Matthias to join them from Baltimore. Ruth had dinner with Matthias, and his surrogate father did what fathers are supposed to do: He delivered a personal sermon to the Babe on the evil of his ways. Ruth took it to heart, at least for a while. His marriage to Helen was definitely over, the Sudbury farm had been sold, and she and Dorothy had moved to Boston. The last public appearance of the three together was at that year's World Series.

In that fall classic, the Yankees faced the Cardinals, another offensive powerhouse, led by player-manager Rogers Hornsby, perhaps the greatest right-handed hitter of all time. Game 1, however, was a pitcher's duel between Redbird Billy Sherdel and Yank Herb Pennock. The score was tied 1-all in the last of the sixth when Ruth led off with a single, was bunted to second by Meusel, and scored the winning run on

Along with cracking bats and thunderous crowds, the backstop had its quiet moments for Babe and Lou Gehrig.

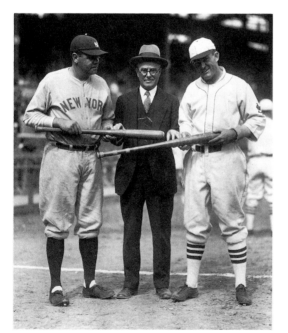

Gehrig's single. In Game 2, the 39-year-old alcoholic, epileptic pitching legend Grover Cleveland ("Pete") Alexander held the Yanks to four hits and won 6-2. The teams moved to St. Louis, and Jesse Haines mastered the Yanks in Game 3, shutting them out on five hits.

Game 4 was the stuff of legend. The first two Yanks struck out, but Babe slugged a home run off Flint Rhem on the first pitch he saw. He homered again in the third inning.

This game, sent over the airwaves through a 33-station radio network, was the first Series game ever broadcast na-

Two of the greatest hitters of all time, Ruth and Rogers Hornsby, square off for the '26 Series.

tionally. Booming-voiced Graham MacNamee's call when Ruth batted again in the sixth against Hi Bell was truly exciting and is worth repeating, for several apparent reasons. MacNamee's words follow.

"The Babe is up. Two home runs today . . . Babe's shoulders look as if there is murder in them down there, the way he is swinging that bat. . . . That great big bat of Babe's looks like a toothpick down there, he is so big himself. . . . Three and two. The Babe is waving that wand of his over the plate. Bell is loosening up his arm. The Babe hits it clear into the centerfield bleachers for a home run! For a home run! Did you hear what I said? Where is that fellow who told me not to talk about Ruth anymore? Send him up here. Oh, what a shot! Directly over second. . . . Oh, what a shot! Directly over second base far into the bleachers out in center field, and almost on a line and then that

True to form, Babe smacks another dinger in the 1926 fall classic.

dumbbell, where is he, who told me not to talk about Ruth! Oh, boy! Not that I love Ruth, but, oh, how I love to see a shot like that! Wow! That is a World Series record, three home runs in one World Series game, and what a home run! That was probably the longest hit ever made in Sportsman's Park. They tell me this is the first ball ever hit in the centerfield stands. That is a mile and a half from here. You know what I mean."

Ruth scored four runs and drove in four as the Yankees romped to a 10-5 win. Another pitchers' duel ended after 10 innings the next day with the Yankees on top 2-1. The teams returned to Yankee Stadium for Game 6, and Alexander spun his magic again, holding Ruth hitless and winning 10-2.

Babe takes time out from slugging for a picture at Athletic Field in October of 1926.

Game 7 was a struggle. Babe's third-inning homer gave the Yankees a one-run lead, but the

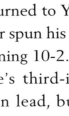

With a narrow Series loss in 1926, the Yanks would soon put their disappointment behind them.

Cards pushed across three in the top half of the fourth. Receiving his ninth walk of the Series in the fifth didn't help Ruth, even though it broke his old Series record. (He would walk twice more in the game.) A run in the sixth brought the Yanks within one.

In the last of the seventh, Combs led off with a single and was bunted to second. Ruth was intentionally passed, and after a force-out, Gehrig also walked, loading the bases with two down. Hornsby called in the rocky veteran Alexander to pitch to the rookie Lazzeri. (Lazzeri, coincidentally, also had epilepsy.) Some said that Pete had celebrated his win the day before a little too much and was severely hungover or maybe even still drunk. Hornsby stared into Pete's eyes and was satisfied with what he saw. Without having thrown a pitch in the bullpen (to conserve the energy left in his aging arm), Alexander struck Lazzeri out.

Pete made quick work of the three Yankees he faced in the eighth and had put the first two down in the ninth when Ruth came to bat. Pitching carefully to the slugger, Pete walked him on a 3-2 count. Alexander was sure that the pitch the ump called ball three was really strike three. He felt the same about ball four. After one strike to Meusel, Ruth lit out on an attempted steal of second. Bob O'Farrell threw him out easily, ending the Series with a stunning surprise.

Although Ed Barrow and others felt Ruth's attempt was a stupid play, Ruth didn't. His logic makes sense: Getting into scoring position with two out would greatly help New York's chances of tying the game. In addition, Ruth wasn't slow; he had swiped 11 bases dur-ing the season, and he had already stolen one base against O'Farrell the day before. Although this was the Yankees' third World Series loss in four appearances, they would win eight more before they lost again.

No slouch on the basepaths, the Babe had stolen 11 bases during the 1926 season. He also wasn't afraid to challenge the opposing fielders' arms to make exciting plays like this one.

One of the most enduring stories created by sportswrit-ers about Ruth had its origins during this Series. A sick boy named Johnny Sylvester lay on his deathbed, severely injured in a fall from a horse. Ruth visited him in the hospital and promised to hit a home run for the dying boy that day. That was the afternoon Ruth slugged not one, not two, but three homers. The boy recovered, and someone decided that Ruth's home run prowess had saved little Johnny's life. Years later, the now-grown boy showed up and thanked the Babe for all he had done, and the two wept in joy.

Great story, but the facts are these. Sylvester's dad wired Ruth from New Jersey, where the family lived, during the Series and asked for an autographed ball. The Yanks and Cards each sent one along. The sick kid was grateful, although no one promised him a home run. After the Series, while Ruth was barnstorming, he showed up at the Sylvester's home one day on an impulse. Ruth and Johnny chatted. A year later, Johnny's uncle met Ruth and thanked him for all he had done for the sickly little lad. The Babe smiled graciously and asked how Johnny was doing. He then turned to a friend and said, "Now who . . . [is] Johnny Sylvester?"

That year's barnstorming routine was a hit. Ruth also performed as a solo act in vaudeville on a 12-week tour that earned him $65,000.

The 1927 season that followed brought its own phenomenon. They called it "Five O'Clock Lightning," and for a very good reason. The 1927 Yankees were known to strike hard and with vengeance in the fifth or sixth inning every day. By this point in the game, they had had the opportunity to familiarize themselves with the other team's starting pitcher, and the pitcher began to tire (even just a little). Unlike baseball today, when the manager will call in a fresh arm as soon as he detects the slightest weakness in his starter or if he can gain a lefty-righty advantage, pitchers in the 1920s were expected to go the full nine. The exception to this was if they were getting their brains beat in, at which point the manager took them out just so they'd rest a little longer before their next start. The concept of the relief specialist was still a few years away, but it was has-

In 1927, the hard-working home run king would scale to new statistical heights.

tened into existence by the powerful Yankees. They were sure to splash their lightning across the sky against any starter who was there too long. Some historians have stated that the development of a solid relief-pitching corps was Babe Ruth's second greatest contribution to baseball strategy.

It was a big money year for Ruth. Before the season he inked a three-year contract worth $70,000 a year. Ed Barrow, the team's general manager, was being paid $25,000. Manager Huggins was earning a little more than half of what Ruth made. No other player earned $20,000. Of course, the baseball salary was only part of Ruth's income. In February 1927, he acted in a movie called *The Babe Comes Home*, which contributed to the estimated $250,000 he made in the year before the 1927 season. To help pay for Ruth's salary, the Yankees didn't have days of rest. Exhibition games were scheduled almost every day that there were no league contests, and Ruth played in nearly every one.

The Bustin' Babes, the slugger's barnstorming team, gave even more opportunities for fans to meet their hero.

The '27 Yanks ran away with the pennant. The second-place A's had the same record New York had won with in 1926 (91-63). In 1927, though, that was only good enough to finish 19 games back. The Yanks' 110-win total was five more than any AL team had ever achieved. Many today still claim that there has never been a greater team than the 1927 Yankees. It's a case that isn't hard to make.

Of the eight American Leaguers to drive in 100 runs in 1927, four were Yankees. The New Yorkers scored 130 runs more than the next highest-scoring team. One team hit more doubles; no team had more hits, triples, homers, walks, a higher batting average, on-base percentage, or slugging average. The Yankees struck out 180 times more than any other club, but so what? They hit 102 more home runs than any other team. One out of every four homers hit in the league that year were hit by Babe Ruth and Lou Gehrig.

With no pennant chase to stir fan interest, the real excitement in the American League in 1927 was the Home Run Derby between Ruth and Gehrig, as each mounted assaults on Ruth's record of 59 homers in a single season. Newspapers fol-

Babe and Lou suit up for a very different look. They flank Knute Rockne, football great, and Christy Walsh, marketing wizard.

lowed the two closely, reporting on which of the big men had slugged one (or more) out that day. In July, Ruth smacked a line drive double off Hod Lisenbee of the Senators that nearly crucified the pitcher as he leaped out of the way. Ruthian mythology altered the facts slightly, claiming that the hit went between the pitcher's legs before it rose on a line and left the park.

As of August 10, Gehrig had 38 homers, Ruth 35. Both had an excellent chance to set a new record, but Gehrig cooled off and Ruth caught fire. The first baseman rapped only nine more; the Babe hit 25.

With four games to go, Ruth needed four homers to break his old mark. He hit one off Lefty Grove on September 27—a grand slam. The next game he hit two, one a bases-empty shot, the other another grand slam. In his third at bat that game, he walloped a triple to center that would have been number 60 if he had only hit it to right. His next time up he rapped a long fly to right, and Goose Goslin had to scrunch himself against the wall to reach up and make the homer-saving catch. Ruth had tied his old record with two games to go.

September 30: The score was even at two when Mark Koenig hit a one-out eighth-inning triple. The Senators could have opted to walk Ruth intentionally and hope for a double play. Pitcher Tom Zachary, however, figured he could get Ruth out. Ruth deposited the third pitch into the rightfield bleachers. Zachary screamed that it was

A couple of "keeds" take some raps at the park.

Here's a moment for the books. In 1927, Babe sent a record number of four-baggers skyward. This is an action shot of number 60.

He was the talk of the town. This cover of New York World *captures the Bambino coming out of the box after blasting one.*

foul; he was overruled. Ruth had broken his own record, and it would stand for 34 years until another New York Yankees right-fielder would almost crack under the strain of trying to top it.

The Yankees' 1927 World Series opponents were the Pittsburgh Pirates, who, unlike the Yanks, had to fight through a tough pennant race, winning by just a game and a half. The Pirates as a team posted a batting average just two points less than New York's (.305 to .307), and they also topped their league in hits and runs scored. Lacking in their lineup, however, were any big bangers like Ruth, Gehrig, and Lazzeri. Three future Hall of Famers were in the Bucs' starting lineup: Pie Traynor and the Waner brothers, Paul and Lloyd. Their pitching staff had two starters who wore glasses—a rarity for the times.

The Ruth myth for that year was invented by one of Christy Walsh's ghostwriters. It said that the Pirates, while watching pre-Series batting practice, were awed by the Yankees size and power and were therefore crushed by the dominating Yanks in four games. The truth, however, is quite different.

The dirt-tough Pirates were not a team that was easily scared, for one. For another, no Pirate that historians have ever interviewed recalls having watched that batting practice. The Yanks won in four games, all right, but the scores were 5-4, 6-2, 8-1 (featuring a one-inning six-run outburst), and 4-3. In fact, the Yankees won the last game when Pirates pitcher John Miljus ("The Big Serb") threw two wild pitches in the same inning.

After the Series, the barnstorming teams of "The Larrupin' Lou's" and "The Bustin' Babes" played 21 games. Ruth had originally planned to give Gehrig a percentage of the gate as his pay but rethought the matter and paid Lou a flat $10,000. It was $3,000 more than Gehrig had earned for the entire regular season. In typical fashion, 13 of the games were never finished because fans poured down out of the stands and took over the field.

About this time, the relationship between Ruth and Gehrig began to change. The young Gehrig was originally one of those who sat at the feet of the great Bambino and adored his every move. As Gehrig matured, however, he began to stand up to Ruth. There were verbal spats between the pipe-smoking, college-educated Lou and the ebullient, stogie-chomping Babe. On the field they were cordial, even friendly (the look on Lou's face as Babe touches home after his "called shot" homer in the 1932 World Series is one of childish delight), but their lifestyles and manners were too different to allow much else.

The 1927 Yankees. This collection of dynamite put together some explosive games.

The pairing of Babe and Lou made for a fantastic barnstorming tour.

To the delight of everyone in Dexter Park, the Sultan and the Crown Prince doff their 10-gallon hats to the admiring crowd.

For awhile their children played together, but one day Gehrig's mother made a rude comment that Dorothy, the Ruths' adopted daughter, wasn't dressed as well as Julia, Claire's offspring. Claire heard of it and was outraged. When she told the Babe, so was he. Ruth sent a message to Gehrig the next day: "Don't ever speak to me again off the ball field." The natural rivalry between the two ballplaying geniuses turned into something quite personal and ugly. (In her biography, Claire takes full responsibility for the chill between the two great players, saying she overreacted.) Ruth and Gehrig would pose for pictures as courteous teammates, but their relationship was solid ice.

They didn't make up until Lou Gehrig Appreciation Day in 1939, the day of the dying Lou's famous "I'm the luckiest man on the face of the earth" speech. After he finished speaking, he turned to look, almost as if for approval, to his estranged former teammate (by this time Ruth was out of baseball). The Babe responded by giving Lou a giant hug.

As had now become his offseason routine, Ruth put himself under the brutal supervision of Artie McGovern for grueling daily workouts to get himself in shape. McGovern claimed, "Ruth is physically five to 10 years younger than he was two years ago [when they first began the workouts]." The Babe still indulged himself, but now in new pastimes like bridge, fox hunting (he could sweat off five pounds in one day on the horses), and the saxophone. It is known that he mastered one song; whether he ever learned a second is unknown. One vice did

not go away; he still couldn't keep his heavy foot off the gas pedal. He was arrested for speeding again in May.

With the exception of signing promising young catcher Bill Dickey and obtaining Leo Durocher as a fill-in infielder, the nucleus of the Yanks remained unchanged for the 1928 season. The pitching staff needed some shuffling. Urban Shocker, the 37-year-old pitcher who had won 18 games for the '27 squad, found his heart condition was too debilitating and left the club during spring training. He died that September. Illness also hampered Herb Pennock's effectiveness; George Pipgras took over, and Waite Hoyt remained consistent.

The Yankees opened the season by trouncing the Philadelphia A's and never looked back. By Independence Day in July, they were 13½ games in front of Philadelphia. When the first of August rolled around, Ruth had hit 42 homers, putting him 26 games ahead of his 60-homer 1927 pace. (As it would turn out, he would hit just a dozen more.)

Injuries began to pester the Yanks. A shoulder problem forced Lazzeri out of the lineup, making the acquisition of the feisty Durocher (whom Ruth never liked, thinking him a dandy) especially valuable. The seemingly unstoppable scoring machine was getting stopped more and more frequently. Mean-

Bam goes the Bambino, and out flies another. In 1928, he again led the league in a multitude of categories. His 54 homers were good for the top rung.

Quit monkeying around! It seems that the Babe never refused a photo opportunity.

Fans litter the field with hats to show their jubilation after the Babe clouts another circuit smash.

while, the Athletics were on their way to becoming one of the great teams of the century. The energetic young A's drove forward while the vaunted Yanks stumbled.

Like its superstar outfielder, however, this Yankees team had a flair for the dramatic. By September 9, in a New York doubleheader between the two teams, the A's had moved into first place by half a game. There were 8,000 standing room only tickets put on sale that day; 25,000 people tried to buy them. Special police units had to be called in to quell the bedlam. Attendance was quoted as 85,265. (Yankee Stadium had been enlarged in the offseason.) The Yanks swept Philadelphia that day, and after an off-day Ruth untied the next game in the eighth with a two-run homer off supreme hurler Lefty Grove. The *New York Times* said, "It was the Ruth, the whole Ruth, and nothing but the Ruth at Yankee Stadium yesterday." Even though the race wasn't technically over, the Philadelphia spirit was crushed. The Yanks ended the season 2½ games in front.

The home run king.

However, once those games were played, Ruth stopped hitting entirely. Historian Lee Allen described the scene perfectly: "A large man in a camel's-hair coat and camel's-hair cap, standing in front of a hotel, his broad nostrils sniffing at the promise of the night." Huggins considered another severe suspension and fine, but rethought it when he realized he would be laughed at. His team was in first place, after all.

The pennant-clinching celebration in Detroit was riotous. Ruth wanted a piano, but the hotel couldn't find one. So the Babe bought one and had it delivered.

While their spirits were high, physically the Yankees were in sad shape. Koenig, Ruth, Gehrig, Dugan, and Lazzeri were all below par with an assortment of injuries. Herb Pennock didn't pitch after August because of a sore arm. Earle Combs racked up his wrist two days before the end of the season. With those facts in hand and the memory of the Yankees slump in mind, those who were inclined to predict felt that the Cardinals (now managed by Bill McKechnie) would handle the Yankees easily in the World Series. The odds-makers put it at 6-5, Cards.

The Babe Ruth Candy Company was one of his many business ventures.

The difference between the '26 Cardinals and their '28 counterpart was one of managerial philosophy. While Rogers Hornsby had decided to keep the ball away from Ruth, walking him 11 times, McKechnie favored pitching to the big guy. It was a major tactical mistake.

In the first three games, the Yankees outscored the Cardinals 20-7. Ruth had seven hits and had scored six runs. In the fourth game, the Yanks were down 2-1 when "Five O'Clock Lightning" struck in the seventh inning. Pitcher Billy Sherdel tried to "quick pitch" Ruth. The move, legal in the National League but not in the American (and vetoed for Series play by Landis), was ruled no pitch. The St. Louis fans and players were outraged. Several loud debates with the umpires roared around the field. Babe walked around the arguing clusters of men with a broad grin on his face. Once they settled down, he did something he would be given more credit for a few years later. Ruth barked at Sherdel, "Put one right here and I'll knock it out of the park." Sherdel took the bait. Ruth hit the ball over the rightfield pavilion. Gehrig followed with another homer,

Is it the sweet sound of success or just a sour note? Paying no heed to Lou's dismay, Babe wails on the sax like there's no tomorrow.

The 1928 Champions take time out for a team snapshot at Detroit's Navin Field.

and the Yanks put up two more runs before the inning was over. They added another deuce in the eighth off old-timer Pete Alexander, propelled by Ruth's third homer of the game.

The game belonged to the Babe. So he decided to end it with a final Ruthian fillip. The Cards scored once in the last of the ninth and had two men on when Frank Frisch lofted a foul fly down the leftfield line. Ruth charged over and snagged the ball on a dead run before it could fall into the temporary seats. Then he held it proudly aloft for all to see as he hustled into the dugout.

The storytellers claim that the 1927 Series was a Yankee blowout; that is incorrect. The 1928 Series, by contrast, definitely was. The team celebrated in full Yankees style. Ruth kept the train from leaving the station until he was sure there were enough supplies for the party to come en route, including four bushels of spare ribs. All the way from St. Louis to New York that night, whenever the train passed through a small town, throngs of people gathered and cheered to see the Babe. He made dozens of appearances from the back of the train on the way home, with varying degrees of politeness. The crowds loved it anyway.

On January 11, 1929, Helen Ruth died. She had been living for several years with a Watertown, Massachusetts, dentist, and most people thought they were husband and wife. A fire ravaged the house where she lived. Unable to escape, she perished in the blaze. When her true identity was discovered, it was a national sensation. The Babe wept openly at her funeral service.

At one point during 1929 spring training, Miller Huggins was arrested in Daytona, Florida, suspected of being a hotel burglar. The tightly wrapped Huggins had difficulty persuading the local constabulary of his innocence, not to mention his true identity. The ball club thought it a hoot. On the field, the potent Yanks kept strutting their stuff. They won 16 of their 24 games and scored 201 runs.

Huggins wasn't satisfied; he noticed a new smugness among his team. His charges weren't playing with the necessary intensity; they were basking in their suc-

The Babe mourns at Helen's funeral. Helen's sister and mother are on either side of him.

cess. "They turn to the financial pages first and the sports pages later," he explained.

April 17 was the scheduled Opening Day. That morning Babe and Claire Hodgson were married. While the game was rained out, the Ruths had a day of honeymoon before the season got underway. In the rescheduled opener, the Yankees were attired in their new uniforms: pinstriped, because natty dresser Colonel Ruppert felt the stripes would make Babe's large middle less obvious, and with their numbers on the back, the first team ever to do so. Wearing number 3 (according to his spot in the batting order), Babe swatted a homer that nearly landed in Claire's lap in the leftfield stands.

Claire was the third person to make a positive difference in Babe Ruth's life, after the paternal Brother Matthias and the dollar-wise Christy Walsh. Ruth settled down with the beautiful, no-nonsense Claire and became a devoted husband and father. He and Claire adopted Dorothy. Claire watched over the Babe with keen, attentive eyes. She made him dress better (or at least less garishly). She traveled with the team, even though the Ruths had to pay for it out of their own pocket. On the

Former star of the stage, Claire Hodgson, marries George Herman Ruth at an early morning ceremony on April 17, 1929.

road she saw that Babe ate dinners with her in their hotel suites; at home she watched his diet. She kept him on a schedule so he was certain to get enough sleep. Claire was very protective of her Babe, forbidding him to lift any heavy objects, even his suitcase. He was not allowed to touch can openers and razor blades. Instead, he went to the barber for his daily shave.

She set a routine. Every year she threw a huge New Year's Eve Party, and the next day Ruth gave up hard liquor and headed for Artie McGovern's gym. Only beer was allowed in their home from January 1 through the end of the World Series. She also acted as Babe's personal secretary. It is said she was highly amused by the many phone calls to Babe from aggressively adoring young ladies.

Best of all, Claire helped cool Ruth's extravagant spending. If he needed money, he had to ask Claire for a $50 check. Gone were the days of hundred dollar tips and diamond gifts to casual acquaintances. Of course, sometimes she had to write a fistful of $50 checks on a single day, but that was much better than Ruth's previous habit of carrying around thousands of dollars, yet always being broke. With Claire's tight rein on the purse strings and Walsh's investments, it didn't take long for the Babe to become financially set for life. On the field, though, his team was slipping. Historically it's almost a baseball axiom that a team which is traditionally strong in

Two longball specialists await their turn to knock some out.

one area (offense, defense, or pitching) will overrate the importance of that area and underrate the rest. The Yankees had some excellent pitchers during the Ruth glory years, but Yankees scoring explosions could make any pitcher look better than he was. By 1929, their five top pitchers were all close to 30 years old. Since the Red Sox well had dried up, the Yankees pitching staff hadn't been buoyed by young new talent. In 1929, the Yankees scored 899 runs. Only three times in the previous 30 years had a team in either league reached that level of offensive potency. Twice it had been Ruth's team. Ruth belted 46 homers to lead the league; Gehrig swatted 35. Ruth drove in 154 runs, Gehrig 126, and Lazzeri 106. Lazzeri hit .354; the Babe .345. Pitching was the Yankee Achilles' heel. The staff allowed almost three-quarters a run per game more than the top pitching team in the league—the Philadelphia Athletics.

Connie Mack's club was one of the truly greatest teams of all time. They had powerful hitters: Jimmie Foxx at first, Mickey Cochrane at catcher, and an outfield that consisted of Bing Miller, Mule Haas, and Al Simmons, who batted .335, .313, and .365, respectively. Combined they added 58 homers and 332 RBIs. In addition, they had what the Yankees did not—superb pitching. Their staff was led by Lefty Grove, George Earnshaw, Rube Walberg, and Eddie Rommel.

The A's made the pennant race a runaway. The Yanks finished second, but they were 18 games back. The only real excitement for Yan-

Newlyweds Babe and Claire at the opening of the 1929 season.

Going, going, gone! The slugger sends another one out of the park.

Lou and the Babe were sweeping the baseball world. Here they are pictured together on the cover of The Sporting News Record Book for 1929.

kees fans took place in Cleveland on August 11, when Babe belted his 500th career homer.

The simple fact is, that at age 34, Babe Ruth's remarkable physical skills were waning. All the sweat in McGovern's gym couldn't prevent the inevitable. In 1929, Ruth appeared in just 135 games, the fewest since he became a Yankee, with the exception of the suspension year and the bellyache season.

The crumbling Yankees fortunes were taking their toll on Manager Huggins. The slight skipper, who suffered from a variety of painful ailments his entire life, came down with erysipelas, a disease which affects the entire body but is notably marked by severe inflammation of the tissue under the skin. Early in September, the manager tried an old-fashioned clubhouse pep talk to spark his team.

They were blasè. By September 22, his condition had worsened so much that he checked into the hospital. He died three days later. When the New York clubhouse heard the announcement of their manager's death, the ever-emotional Ruth wept.

With Huggins gone, however, Ruth saw the opportunity to realize a highly powerful personal dream. He wanted to be the manager of the Yankees. He asked Barrow but was rejected. The Yankees instead turned to their former pitcher and current coach, Bob Shawkey. Unlike the irascible and dyspeptic Huggins, Shawkey was a quiet and gentle man noted for both his pitching skills and also his ability to teach young hurlers. He seemed like the perfect choice for a pitching-poor team tired of Huggins's snappish style. Ruth grudgingly agreed that his former teammate deserved the job. Ruth and Claire headed south to spring training in St. Petersburg, but Ruth had not yet signed a con-

tract. He had made $70,000 a year under his old one, and wanted $100,000; Ruppert offered a $5,000 raise to $75,000. Ruth surprisingly responded that it wasn't the money; it was the principle. Christy Walsh composed a letter for him which asserted that if Ruth quit baseball at that moment, he'd still make $25,000 a year for life because of his investments and endorsements. The braggadocio made loud news in the press. Ruth relaxed his demand to $85,000 a year for three years; Ruppert offered $80,000 a year for two.

While he didn't always connect, mighty Babe was always exciting to watch.

Meanwhile, Ruth kept playing during spring training. Until, that is, one of the writers following the Yankees pointed out that the Babe's bargaining position would greatly deteriorate if he were hurt while playing. Babe got the message. He announced that unless Ruppert came through with an $85,000 contract by noon the next day, Ruth would quit baseball forever. Now the newspapers were boiling with the inflammatory news.

Never one to worry about what the papers wrote about him, Ruth abruptly changed his mind the next morning and signed on Ruppert's terms by noon. When someone pointed out that now Babe was making more than Herbert Hoover, president of the United States, he commented, "So what? I had a better year." He was right. In addition, Ruppert rebated the $5,000 Ruth felt Huggins had unjustly fined him in 1925. The 1930 Yankees got off to a slow start under their new manager. Ruth was injured several times during April. He hurt his foot

The frustrations of competition can get to anyone. Shortly after the Bambino voices his displeasure to the official, the ump sends him to the showers.

Jackie Mitchell, who struck out Ruth and Gehrig, as she appeared in 1931.

sliding into third, and when he tried to score on a fly ball by the next hitter, he knocked himself cold diving into home. It took four men to tote him off the field.

On May 21, Ruth came to the plate in Shibe Park in Philadelphia and clouted three home runs in his first three at bats. No one in major league baseball had hit four homers in a game since 1896. (The four-homer feat is still more rare than pitching a perfect game.) For some inexplicable reason, Ruth decided to bat righthanded his last time up, and against a righthanded pitcher at that. After two strikes he jumped back to the lefty side and struck out.

Shawkey's personality wasn't meshing with those of his players. Some of the New York Yankees openly felt Ruth should have been named manager and undermined the easygoing Shawkey. Shawkey and star pitcher Waite Hoyt didn't see eye to eye, and Hoyt and Koenig were dealt to the Tigers at the end of May. The Yankees went on a tear that moved them to within 2.5 games of the Athletics, but when Ruth tried to snag a long fly ball before it left the park, he ripped off a fingernail on the wire fence. The Yankees ended the season 16 games back. Shawkey was fired and replaced by Joe McCarthy, who had been dumped by the Cubs with four games left in the season. (Interestingly, McCarthy, who never played a day in the majors, had been the second batter Babe pitched to as a professional in 1914.)

Again, Ruth let it be known to Ruppert, Barrow, and anyone else within earshot that he felt he deserved a chance to be the Yankees manager. He and some of his teammates openly questioned why New York would hire a National Leaguer to manage them.

The big news of that year's spring training was the feat of female pitcher Jackie Mitchell striking out Ruth and Gehrig back-to-back in an exhibition game. The accomplishment was discredited a bit as the event had the feel of a publicity-boosting charade.

On Opening Day in 1931, Ruth tried to score from third on a short fly ball and collided furiously at home with sturdy Boston catcher Charlie Berry, a former All-American football player. Babe returned to the outfield for the next inning but collapsed in pain shortly thereafter when he tried to chase down a fly ball. Nerves in his thigh were paralyzed. His injuries were serious enough that he had to be hospitalized and missed 10 days.

The Yankees were never in the 1931 pennant race, falling behind Philadelphia and Washington early in the season. As the year wore on, however, they began to click under new manager McCarthy. By June 1, they were eight games over .500;

Even though the 1930 Yankees finished in third at 16 games back, Ruth and Gehrig placed in the top five of many categories. Some felt a different manager would have made the difference in the club's performance.

The 1931 version of Murderer's Row. While this group did not achieve the success of their counterparts in 1927, they were still a force to be reckoned with.

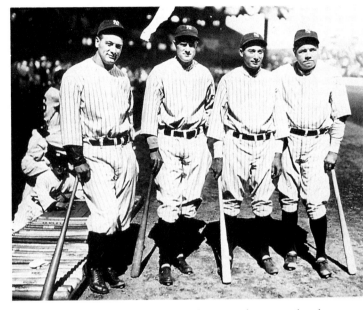

Holiday greetings from the Bambino.

I take my Bat in hand - -
Babe Ruth

one month later, they were 17 over. By the end of the year they had sneaked past Washington to finish second, 13½ games out. At the core of their steady improvement were two significant factors.

One was the emergence of Lefty Gomez as a star pitcher. The rookie went 21-9. The other was the way the strict discipline of Joe McCarthy took effect. McCarthy set inflexible rules: His team had to wear jackets and ties on the road, and every player had to arrive for breakfast in the dining room by 8:30 in the morning. (The Babe, of course, was excused. If he showed up in a public eating place, the crowds would overwhelm the situation.) McCarthy's toughness was always fair, and it worked. In 30 years of minor and major league managing, McCarthy-led teams would finish in the second division only once; his lifetime managerial winning percentage, .614, is the highest ever.

Offensively, the Yanks were back to their old form, leading the American League in hits, runs, homers, RBIs, walks, batting average, on-base percentage, and slugging average. At age 36, Ruth batted .373, second in the league. Gehrig and Ruth tied for the home run lead with 46 long balls. Gehrig set the all-time American League record with 184 RBIs. The problem, again, was Yankees pitching. Only one pinstripe hurler (besides Gomez, who appeared in more than 18 games and had an ERA of 2.63) managed an ERA below 4.28.

On August 21, in St. Louis, Ruth hit his 600th career home run. At $80,000, Ruth made twice as much as any other active player. Next was playing manager

Rogers Hornsby. (It is said that Ty Cobb made $80,000 in 1927 as an Athletic.) Now, though, Ruth was not the free-spending person he had once been. Sportswriters marveled at how he became the unofficial financial consultant for the other Yankees; the man who had been the team (and world) leader in expensive hijinks was now offering free advice on the wisdom of investing in trust funds.

That December, Ruth played Santa Claus for 300 kids at city hospitals. When a reporter asked him to describe his "greatest feat" of 1931, Ruth candidly replied, "Shooting a 73 at St. Alban's golf course in December."

Two Babes are better than one seems to be the thought behind this pairing. Babe Didrikson Zaharias teams up with you know who for a charity golf outing.

While the Babe was enjoying the rewards from his well-handled income, the Depression was deepening for the rest of the nation. Baseball's owners, who had livened up the ball for the 1930 season and promptly set attendance records, de-juiced the ball for 1931. American League home runs fell by nearly 100; the league batting average plummeted 10 points. Not surprisingly, attendance fell, too. There was method to the owners' madness. Players with lower batting averages could not demand higher salaries. Crying poor-mouth, the owners set out on a cost-cutting spree for the 1932 season. Even Judge Landis took a salary reduction—from $65,000 to $50,000. The Yankees wanted to slice off a sizable chunk of Babe Ruth's salary, too—$10,000—to $70,000. The disingenuous avarice of such a move is absolutely beyond reason. Ruth was still the game's largest drawing card, the biggest profit-making machine

Even with fewer home runs league-wide due to altering the make-up of the ball, the Babe's fandom continued to grow.

Babe Ruth: His Life and Times

Ruth continued his workouts at Artie McGovern's gym before spring training. Shown here on the treadmill, the Babe is under the watchful eye of Artie himself.

any team would ever have. In an un-guarded moment, Colonel Huston once es-timated that Ruth added, on the average, 2,500 paying admissions to every game. One commentator calculated that that meant an additional $280,000 per season to the Yankees. A contemporary writer took out his abacus and stated, "Ruth [has] earned $3,500,000 for Colonel Ruppert in the last twelve years . . . over and above what the club would have taken in with-out him." Another averred that the money Ruth brought in from exhibition games (regular and preseason) alone had been enough to pay his salary every year since 1927. Ruth, in a less acquisitive mood than he had been two years earlier, signed a blank contract, which Ruppert filled in with $75,000, plus a bonus of 25 percent of the *net* receipts of exhibition games.

Ben Chapman, Babe Ruth, and Earle Combs in 1932.

After 19 years as a professional athlete, Babe's body was really beginning to suf-fer from the wear and tear. All season long he put up with leg problems: a charley horse here, a sprain there. The ancient cartilage tear in his knee resurfaced with frequent pain. He ripped a muscle in the back of his leg in July and sat out nearly two weeks. The leg pains were so severe that Ruth quit playing golf, one of his favorite pastimes, during the sea-son. In September he had what he thought was an appendicitis attack; the doctors did not operate, but they kept him packed in ice for three days. (Showing his sense of humor

10 days after the icing, he said, "I still haven't thawed out.") Frequently during the season Ruth was removed late in the game for a pinch runner or defensive substitute. Sammy Byrd and Myril Hoag therefore earned themselves the nickname of "Babe Ruth's legs."

Even with Ruth hobbled, the 1932 Yankees would not be denied. They scored the almost incomprehensible total of 1,002 runs (no team had ever done that before; only two other teams have since). That works out to an average of six and a half runs per game. Ruth hit 41 homers, Gehrig 34. In one memorable June game, Gehrig hit four homers and Ruth one in a 20-13 Yank victory. Ruth didn't win the home run crown; Philadelphia's Jimmie Foxx did. Foxx also outslugged Ruth; it was only the second time since 1917 that Babe Ruth had not led the league in that category. The A's also took over the traditional Yankee titles of team leadership in batting average and slugging percentage. For a change, the New Yorkers' pitching was in top form. Lefty Gomez, now 23, put up his second

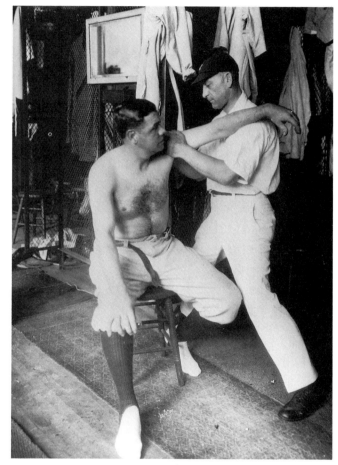

Despite his preseason efforts, the slugger's body needed more attention than before. The many years of physical use had really begun to take their toll.

consecutive 20-win season; Red Ruffing won 18; Johnny Allen, 17, and George Pipgras, 16. More importantly, the Yankee staff as a whole led the league in earned run average. The Yanks jumped into first place in late May and ended the season 13 games in front of Philadelphia. It would have been impossible for a team to lead the league in ERA and score a thousand runs and not win the pennant. Their World Se-

Claire keeps a watchful eye on the legal documents that her Bambino is signing. Colonel Ruppert (far right) makes sure everything is in proper order.

ries opponents that year were a curious bunch. The Chicago Cubs had won the National League flag in 1929 under the leadership of Joe McCarthy (now the Yankees manager). In 1930, with the Cubs only a handful of games behind the St. Louis Cardinals and four games left in the season, McCarthy was dumped and replaced by Rogers Hornsby. Under Hornsby's slash-and-burn personality, the team finished 17 games out of first in 1931, but amazingly "the Rajah" kept his job. The situation would soon change.

He lost it with his team in first place in August of 1932. The Cubs, locked in a tight pennant race with Pittsburgh and Chicago, replaced Hornsby with the kindly ministrations of manager "Jolly Cholly" Grimm (who had once been traded from the Pirates because he played the banjo too much). Historian Bill James has pointed out that when a team is chafing under a strict disciplinarian manager, the best thing ownership can do is hand the players a fun-loving, easygoing sort. The pro-Ruth faction was why this hadn't worked for the Yanks under Shawkey. The Cubs caught fire, spurred by the late-season acquisition of former Yank Mark Koenig, who batted .353 in 31 games for them.

When it came time to vote World Series shares, however, the penurious Chicago Cubs

Ruth congratulates Jimmie Foxx on becoming the home run champ for 1932. Foxx's 54 longballs, however, fell six short of the Babe's 1927 record.

voted Koenig just a half-share, and former manager Hornsby was given nothing. The Yankees, each and every one, thought that was the ultimate in cheapness. As the Series began, they let the Chicagoans know their feelings on the matter.

In comparison, the generous Yanks voted a trainer a three-quarter share and a half-share to Charlie Devens, a rookie who pitched just nine innings that season. In addition to the Koenig-cheapness attitude, the Yank players agreed that McCarthy had been mistreated by Cubs management with his untimely and sudden axing. The riotous badmouthing between the two teams started before the first game and never let up. The Yankees loved calling the Cubs "penny-pinchers," "tightwads," and "skinflints." What the Cubs hollered back isn't printable. One historian said "the tone approach[ed] the style of an Ozark feud more than a professional sporting event." The press even joined in the fray.

As Game 1 began, Guy Bush retired the Yankees order the first time through without anyone reaching base. He walked Earle Combs to open the fourth, a Ruth single drove in the first Yankee run, and Gehrig followed with a home run. Bush fell apart in the sixth, walking four Yanks. By the time the inning was over, New York had a commanding 8-2 lead. They won 12-6.

Cub pitcher Lon Warneke opened Game 2 the way Bush had ended his stint, issuing free passes to the first two Yankees. Two runs came in. Two more walks cost him two more runs in the third, and Lefty Gomez shut out the Cubs the rest of the

This photo of the Babe was taken during Game 2 of the '32 World Series against the Chicago Cubs. No one knew of the excitement and controversy that would follow the next time these two teams met.

Who could refuse such tempting offers?

way. Yankee Stadium was not sold out for this game; the Depression was taking its toll.

Game 3 was one of the rowdiest World Series contests ever. It resulted in one of the largest legends of all time for the largest legend of all time—Babe Ruth.

The Cubs were most likely feeling better as they were heading back to their home park, Wrigley Field in Chicago. Their fans were in a frenzy. It was one of those now-famous Wrigley days when the wind is blowing out, and every pitcher is ducking the ominous sense of impending doom. The fans were already chiding Ruth and the Yankees when batting practice began. Babe stuck their noise back in their faces by slugging nine balls out of the park in practice; Gehrig added seven. In inimitable Babe-style, Ruth shouted at the Cub bench, "I'd play for half my salary if I could hit in this dump all the time." The fans responded by tossing lemons at the Babe, and he playfully tossed them back.

Tempers were hot on both sides, and they didn't cool when Billy Jurges, replacing the injured Koenig, threw wildly on the first ball the Yankees hit in the first inning. Joe Sewell followed with a walk, and Ruth really sent the fans into a tizzy when he casually homered deep into the rightfield bleachers to give New York a 3-0 lead. Lemons poured onto the field as he circled the bases.

In the second inning, Ruth backed Kiki Cuyler to the right field wall. With not an inch to spare, Cuyler snagged Babe's towering fly. Gehrig led off the third with a solo homer, but the Cubs came back to score twice in that inning, then tacked on one in the fourth to tie the game at four each. Understand the situation: A Yank win would put them in the insurmountable position of a 3-0 lead in games. A Cubs win would put them just one victory away from a tie.

In the top of the fifth the Yankees untied the game in a way only the great teams of Ruth could. When the Babe came to bat with one out, both the Cubs bench and the fans were assaulting him with the ugliest verbal abuse. The first pitch by Charlie Root was called a strike. Ruth sarcastically held up one finger, broadly announcing to the world that he definitely knew the count. After two balls another strike was called, and Babe obligingly held up two fingers, quietly stating the fine old baseball cliché, "It only takes one." The Cubs were like madmen in their ferocious screaming at the Babe, and the Yanks were giving it right back. The incensed Guy Bush, out of control, ran part of the way out of the dugout to scream obscenities at Ruth.

What happened next is still being debated today. Ruth was waving his bat and his right hand toward the Cubs dugout, toward the outfield. Some thought he was indicating he'd line the next pitch foul at the Cubs bench. Others surmised that since pitcher Root was shouting at him, Ruth was basically indicating that he was going to knock the next pitch right down the hurler's throat. By now the ballpark was in total

The ol' 3-4 combo strikes again.

bedlam. Ruth was gesturing, the two benches were screaming, and the fans were on the verge of a riot. The stage was set for something dramatic.

Of all times, Root tried to fool the Babe with a slow curve inside. Babe cracked it all the way into the centerfield bleachers, the longest home run anyone could ever

remember at Wrigley. (It was his 15th and last World Series homer.) Gehrig followed with another homer on the next pitch. The Yankees had reasserted their amazing dominance. After the game, one reporter (of the dozens who were there) wrote that Ruth had "called his shot," pointing to the centerfield bleachers before he proceeded to belt the ball out there. No one else had seemed to notice, although Gehrig was quoted, "Did you see what that big monkey did? He said he'd hit a homer, and he did."

Within days the story had spun into legend: Babe Ruth, in a tied World Series game, had called his shot. Ruth, never shy about embellishing his leg-

This artist's rendering depicts a popular opinion on what happened that day in 1932.

end, claimed he had thought about doing just that the night before. Today at the Hall of Fame in Cooperstown you can listen to a tape of Babe Ruth relating the story: "I told him I was going to hit the next pitched ball right into centerfield for a home run."

Did the Babe really "call his shot" in that game? No one can be sure. It is absolutely certain that he always had a flair for the dramatic, from his exuberant catch and toss to end the first game he played in Baltimore in 1914, to his running grab to end the 1928 Series, to his countless clutch home runs. As Roger Kahn said, where the Babe was, center stage was. Ruth said after the Series, "That's the first time I ever got the players and the fans going at the same time. I never had so much fun in my whole life." For a Babe Ruth historian, it may be the ultimate Ruth quote.

A film discovered in 1992 seems to show him pointing to centerfield. But then again, he was making broad gestures just about everywhere. One might look to two people as the voices of authority on the matter, namely those closest to the play: Cubs catcher Gabby Hartnett and pitcher Charlie Root. Hartnett flatly denied Ruth had said any such thing about calling a homer. Root stated unequivocally: "Anyone who knows me knows [that if Ruth had tried that] he would have ended up on his [backside]." The intense battler, Root wasn't kidding. Some 15 years later, when asked to play himself and re-create the scene for the Ruth film biography, he flatly refused.

The world champion 1932 Yankees.

The battle over what truly happened in that one moment of time so long ago may never be settled. Whatever the facts may be, one thing is clear: Babe Ruth, for one of the last times in his life, had done something positively Ruthian. As biographer Tom Meany says, "It was slightly colossal."

Things were no happier for the Cubs as Game 4 began. The first two Yankees singled in the first inning. Ruth was hit on the arm by a wicked fastball from Guy Bush, the insane bench jockey who had nearly stormed from the dugout to chal-

The big guy's mighty weapon.

lenge Ruth in Game 3. Ruth shouted, "Was that your fastball? I thought it was a gnat." However, the injury was serious, and Ruth's arm swelled painfully. He would not have been able to play Game 5. Despite the early advantage, the Yanks could manage just one run (on a mammoth sacrifice fly by Gehrig), and Chicago answered with four runs in the last of the inning.

A two-run homer by Lazzeri in the third and two more Yank runs in the sixth put them in front, but the Cubs replied with a solo tally to even the score. In the seventh, "Five O'Clock Lightning" struck in all its fury. The Yanks powered home four runs, one on a Ruth single, despite his pained arm. Then they did it again in the ninth, with Lazzeri's second two-run homer aiding the cause.

The final was 13-6. The Yankees had won 12 straight World Series games, something no team accomplished before or since. Ruth had provided the most dramatic moment— perhaps the most dramatic of his dramatic career, a moment that will always be a segment in baseball and Ruth history. The times of the Yankees were changing, though; the Ruth era was coming to an end. Gehrig, who was taking over the Ruth mantle of slugging leader, was the real star of the Series, with a .529 batting average (to Ruth's .333), three homers, nine hits, and eight RBI to lead all batters.

"Babe Ruth: The Called Shot"

This promotional card celebrates the "called shot." The slugger sure knew how to get our attention.

1933-1935

Back to Beantown:
Broken Promises, Broken Dreams

"There is no charity in baseball."

**—Colonel Jacob Ruppert,
one–time Yankees owner**

BACK TO BEANTOWN: BROKEN PROMISES, BROKEN DREAMS

Previous page: The Babe hams it up with young fans during a trip to Tokyo.

With the nation reeling from the Crash of '29, baseball, like the rest of the country, was facing changes.

He had emerged in New York at just the right time: America was ready for a new type of hero, and baseball was in need of a savior. Now the country was going through its greatest internal crisis since the Civil War, and a day at the ballpark was seen more as an escape from hard times than as a frivolous adventure. The excesses that had made Babe Ruth so endearing a figure during the Roaring Twenties—his power at bat, his appetite, his gusto for life—no longer seemed quite as magical. Times were changing, and so was the Babe.

Folks had been hardened by the Depression, and photographs from the period show beaten people staring into the camera with eyes that seem at once weary and wise. Many people had lost everything overnight, and the circumstances demanded a new outlook on life and its travails.

What lay ahead for the Babe—from starring in the regal confines of packed Yankee Stadium to struggling before a few shivering fans in cold, sterile Braves Field— did not really seem unusual given the state of the times. It may even, perhaps, have been a validation of reality. If this could happen to the Babe, it really could happen to anybody.

Even after producing one of the most dramatic moments in a career full of them, Ruth had to know he was nearing the end of the line entering the 1933 season. His "called-shot" home run off Chicago's Charlie Root and another World Series win could not hold off advancing age. Babe would later admit in his autobiography that he felt "the old legs were getting tired" as he began his 20th year in the majors.

Babe's 41 homers the previous year had been his lowest since the disastrous 1925 season and broke a string of six straight American League titles in the category. For the first time ever in a season where he played in over 100 games, Ruth failed to lead the league in the statistic that most clearly defined power hitters—slugging percentage. Although he had batted .341 (just one point below his career average and fifth in the league), it was his lowest mark in four years. Not since 1925 had he notched fewer RBI or scored less runs. While his totals of 137 and 120 in those respective categories would be considered spectacular for any other player, in his case they signaled a decline.

While they were all smiles now, Colonel Ruppert and the Babe had some stormy times ahead.

His season record of 60 home runs had been threatened for the first time in 1932, but by a player (Jimmie Foxx) other than himself. Young sluggers like Foxx and Ruth's own teammate Lou Gehrig were now grabbing most of the headlines. After 10 home run titles in 12 seasons, the Babe would never lead the league again. His legs bothered him often, and he was regularly relieved in late innings or the second games of doubleheaders by second-stringers that writers dubbed his "caddies" or "Babe Ruth's legs."

The tide was turning, but there was still time for fun. Ruth followed up the Series with a 10-day November hunting trip to North Carolina with friend and concessionaire magnate Frank Stevens. Babe seemed in grand spirits. He brought three guns, a portable phonograph, and his entire record collection on the excursion, leaving Claire in New York with 30 pounds worth of cakes. (He needed the round tins the baked goods came in to pack his long-playing discs.)

Ruth and daughter Julia mix it up for the cameras.

The trip went well. On one Sunday he shot a turkey for his dinner, then washed it down with roast and boiled ham, potatoes, collards, cake, pie, and a few other goodies. When he returned home to shed his added girth with his annual workouts at Artie McGovern's gym—including some playful sparring with his daughter Julia—he had no idea what was in store for him.

Still the game's highest-paid player, Ruth was learning he was no longer capable of demanding raises while much of the country stood in bread lines. The irony of New York's convincing four-game Series sweep over the Cubs was that Colonel Ruppert and Ed Barrow used it as an excuse to further cut Yankees salaries for '33. Babe was no exception. Barrow estimated that the lack of both a sixth and seventh Series game at the Stadium had cost the club over $100,000 in refunded tickets. Management was also quick to remind players that the Depression gripping the country showed little sign of subsiding.

Even with the repeal of prohibition (and increased beer profits for his brewery) just months away, Ruppert was being more frugal than ever. Whereas the season before Ruth's salary had been cut from its two-year high of $80,000 down to $75,000, his new contract called for $50,000—a cut of 33⅓ percent. Ruth was livid.

Babe takes some time for reflection while nursing a tender ankle.

Shortly after receiving the contract in January, he called Barrow to say he was sending it back. Ed asked him not to go to the newspapers, but a few days later Babe was voicing his gripes in a meeting with reporters.

"I don't mind telling you and the world that the offer is $50,000," he said. "That's a cut of 25 grand, and that's some wallop. I don't believe Colonel Ruppert ever saw the contract, and I told Barrow that. . . . I expected to receive a cut, but I can't believe Jake would go so far as a third off. I'll never sign for that."

Ruppert had seen and approved the cut (although he never admitted this to reporters), and when he ignored Ruth's lamentations, another battle between the two was underway. "I can see a 10 percent cut or even a 15 percent cut," Babe conceded after having time to calm down. "But $25,000 is no cut, that's an amputation." Arguing that even in a Depression year he had helped the Yankees turn a profit by packing the Stadium—where attendance still hovered around one million annually—Ruth left for the South and some golf dates with his old optimism back. "We'll work this out in Florida. We always do."

Times, though, they were a-changing. Fairly or not, Babe could no longer enter negotiations with Ruppert possessing the bargaining power he had in the past. The owner knew he had hitters the likes of Gehrig, Bill Dickey, and Ben Chapman on the roster, and Ruth was clearly not the dominant player he once had been. He still could, however, draw headlines, and as Babe waited out his bosses in Florida yet another rumor began circulating. In big, bold type, some papers reported that he was dead—this time in a plane crash. "Nah, I haven't been in a plane in weeks," a confident Ruth joked. "The worst accident I've had is that Yankees contract."

Ruppert wasn't amused, nor was he budging. After the two started meeting, Ruth eventually offered to come down to $60,000—then $55,000. The exhibition season got underway, and Ruppert's only response was a threat of his own to lower the original offer and not take Ruth north with the team if he remained unsigned by March 29. "I cannot possibly sign him for more than $50,000," the colonel said.

Ruppert could, and did, sign Ruth for more—but the final contract for $52,000 agreed to on March 22 signified a large step in Babe's decline. The Colonel had granted his fading star a concession, but only a slight one; clearly the power in this tug-of-war now belonged to ownership. After all, Ruppert pointed out, Ruth was still the best-paid player in the game. Al Simmons, the great center fielder who had led the A's to three consecutive pennants between 1929 and '31, was making less than $40,000.

For perhaps the first time, some fans found it tough to back the Babe up. Although he had blossomed into baseball's greatest star just when the game needed him, his timing now was off. Folks just didn't want to hear complaints from a guy making over 50 grand, especially when their own money was long gone or tied up in a failed bank.

In typical Ruth fashion, the Bambino provided another one for the record books at the first-ever All-Star Game.

Of course, there were still plenty for whom such circumstances didn't matter in the least. A Salvation Army official asked 1,174 destitute men living in a Manhattan shelter if they could name any Americans who deserved to be making $80,000 (Babe's old salary). When the votes were counted, Ruth trailed only "any President of the United States." Some of the runners-up in this informal survey included a pretty impressive group, among them the likes of President Roosevelt, Professor Albert Einstein, and William Randolph Hearst.

Once the season got underway, Yankees fans had to be wondering if the stocky 38-year-old in right was worth paying at any price. Babe hit just nine homers through May (all but two at home) and was looking appreciably slower in the field. Still, the team now seemed able to win without him; Gehrig and others picked up the slack, and New York took a comfortable lead in the American League race while playing at close to a .700 pace. When Ruth was named in a shared vote of fans and AL man-

ager Connie Mack to start in the first interleague All-Star Game on July 6, many felt it was more a gesture of goodwill than anything else. Ruth's skills had clearly waned even more since the previous season, and his numbers paled in comparison to other sluggers chosen for the game.

President Hoover was one of several leaders that had the opportunity to meet the baseball legend.

Defying logic and the numbers once again, Ruth delighted the 49,200 on hand at Chicago's Comiskey Park for the first midsummer classic. The AL held a 1-0 lead when Ruth came to bat in the third inning with Detroit's Charley Gehringer on base. The Bambino promptly stroked a two-run homer off Bill Hallahan—the first home run in All-Star history. He singled later in the contest, and when Cincinnati's Chick Hafey hit a liner to right in the eighth, Babe made a great running catch to snuff out the final NL rally. The AL claimed a 4-2 victory, with Ruth's hit the game-winner.

Obviously the old man wasn't quite through yet. Babe added eight home runs in July—including three in a doubleheader at Detroit—but now it was the team around him that was slumping. The Senators passed the Yanks to take over first on June 24, and after a brief New York rally, Washington was back in front for good. The pitching-thin pinstripers no longer seemed so imposing to rivals, and Ruth faded in the summer heat with just three August homers. On the third of that month came a moment that perhaps more than any other symbolized the change taking place; when Lefty Grove of the A's shut the Yankees out that afternoon, it

Babe's 1933 Goudy Gum card.

marked the first time in 309 games the Yanks had failed to score at least one run in a contest.

New York wound up in second place with a 91-59 record, seven behind the Senators and a 16-game drop off from the previous season. The year's last game against the Red Sox meant nothing, but for many fans at the Stadium it was probably the most entertaining of the season. Babe was given the start versus Boston, his first pitching assignment since 1930 and only his second in 12 years. Barrow played up the contest as a fitting climax to Ruth's 20th season—what better way to end it than facing the team for whom he had starred as a pitcher? Some 25,000 fans were on hand to watch.

True to old form, baseball's former No. 1 lefty had a 6-0 lead through five innings, thanks in part to his own home run in the fourth. Joe McCarthy asked if he wanted to come out, but Ruth the pitcher had never been one to leave games early. Boston reached him for five singles (four in a row) and four runs in the sixth. Gulping water for strength between each inning, Babe held on for a 6-5 complete-game victory. He had allowed 12 hits (including 11 singles) and developed a stiff and painful arm he couldn't lift for a week, but he had finished what he started. Ruth left the Stadium to polite applause from thousands of fans who had stayed behind. He would never pitch in the majors again.

Since the AL pennant race was basically decided by early September, individual performances like this garnered most of the Yankees spotlight. The most notable of all was turned in by Gehrig, who in August broke Everett Scott's major league mark by playing in his 1,308th consecutive game. The Iron Man had the new record up to 1,350 by season's end and finished with a .352 batting average, 41 doubles, 32 homers, and 139 RBI. The numbers again placed him high among the league leaders (he led everybody with 138 runs scored), and for the first time in his career he actually out-slugged Ruth (.605 to .582).

The Babe was definitely entering the twilight of his career. His 34 homers were two more than his teammate and second in baseball behind AL leader Jimmie Foxx's 48, but the total marked Ruth's first time under 40 since the less-than-stellar "bellyache" season of 1925. A .301 batting average, 103 RBI, and 97 runs were very respectable figures for almost anyone else, but next to the Babe's name they seemed out of place (just as Gehrig's fine 1938 statistics would seem once the effects of the disease that killed him began to set in). Slow and lumbering in the field, Ruth had become a defensive liability; only three of 24 regular outfielders in the American League made fewer putouts than he did, and only eight regulars made fewer errors.

Things had really changed for the Babe. He was no longer the best slug-ger in the game, and he wasn't even the best on his team anymore; that distinction now clearly belonged to first baseman Gehrig. Lou and Jimmie Foxx had become the game's elite power hitters, and by capturing the AL batting, homer, and RBI crowns, Foxx achieved a distinction that had always eluded Ruth—the Triple Crown. When the Baseball Writers' Association of America continued its three-year-old tra-

The King of the Long Ball and the Crown Prince reel in quite a catch while fishing off Fire Island in New York.

dition of naming a Most Valuable Player following the season, the honor went to Foxx for the second consecutive time, with Gehrig finishing fourth. Babe did not receive a single vote.

The Ruth family gets together for a sing-along to celebrate the Babe's 40th birthday.

Ruth had often speculated openly that he would retire following his 20th season, and this certainly seemed like a good time to get out. His skills were reduced but still somewhat respectable. New York had slipped a bit as a team, and more changes would likely be needed before another pennant would fly over Yankee Stadium. He could leave now with his head held high—and nearly 400 more home runs than anyone else in history.

There were, however, some things Ruth still yearned to achieve in the game. He had already accomplished his long-stated goals of playing for 20 years and in 10 World Series, but he still wanted both to hit 700 home runs (he was 14 short) and take over as Yankees manager. The homers would undoubtedly come were he to hang in another year, but the second wish was another story.

Other stars had made the transition to managing successfully, including many with no minor-league apprenticeship. Ty Cobb, Tris Speaker, and Joe Cronin had all been offered the post while still active players, and by 1933 this had become somewhat of a trend: Five of 16 big league clubs employed player-managers. Ruth wanted the same chance, but Yankee bosses—especially Ed Barrow—didn't believe he was the right person to handle such responsibility.

On the surface this doesn't make sense. After he had achieved greatness as both a pitcher and hitter, it could be argued that Ruth was more qualified than anyone to lead a team. Over the course of his career thus far (two decades of playing), he had encountered just about every situation he was likely to face as manager. Possibly just as important, his off-field escapades had declined steadily under the watchful eye of Claire. Yet those same qualities that had endeared him to fans and team-mates over the years—his color, enthusiasm, and lack of regard for convention—seemed now to be working against him.

He couldn't remember signs, it was true—but what player had ever hit better with or without them? He still enjoyed his food, drink, and fun on occasion but had a reputation for the most part as a hard-nose player who knew how to win. Even at his heftiest he had been the best slugger around, and he was slipping now because of age—not accumulated poundage. It was often said by reporters and other play-ers that Ruth never made a baserunning mistake or threw to the wrong man once in his long career. Even if this was an exaggeration, nobody could deny his knowl-edge of the game.

A wild pitch puts the Bambino on his posterior during an exhibition game.

It all seemed to add up to managerial timber, but Barrow felt otherwise. Maybe he was just sick of all the heartaches and salary squabbles Ruth had given him and Colonel Ruppert over the years, but Ed felt no loyalty whatsoever when it came time to reward Babe for making himself and many oth-ers in the organization wealthy. "At no time during the years he was with the club, from 1920 to 1934, was Ruth ever considered a candidate for manager of the Yan-kees," Barrow said in his autobi-ography published after Babe's death.

Never knowing he had no shot at the job, Ruth had first envisioned becoming manager when Miller

Younger players, like Schoolboy Rowe, were filling the ranks of many major-league teams.

Huggins died. The position was given instead to former New York pitcher Bob Shawkey—Barrow's fourth choice—who finished third his one season (1930) before being fired. Once again Ruth thought his chance was at hand, but when the Cubs released '29 pennant-winning skipper Joe McCarthy, the Yanks quickly snatched him up. McCarthy signed a new three-year contract in 1933, and false rumors began circulating that Babe would get the post when it ran out. The naive, trusting Ruth believed them; it seemed he was determined to stay on as an active Yankee player until he got his due.

If anything, his desire to stay in the Bronx probably cost Babe a chance at other managerial openings. Still floundering in the second division, the Red Sox had gone through five managers in six years and were desperately looking for ways to improve both their fortunes and dismal attendance. Bringing back the most popular player in team history would almost guarantee at least the latter, and with this in mind Ruth was supposedly offered the Boston job in 1932. Babe refused, then due to his high-standing with the Yankees (en route to a pennant at the time). When 33-year-old multi-millionaire Tom Yawkey bought the Sox a year later he too apparently wanted Ruth. Just like Barrow, however, Boston General Manager Eddie Collins had reservations about the choice. Collins talked Yawkey out of making an offer, and the Sox wound up going with former Senators pilot Bucky Harris.

Another chance arose when Tigers owner Frank Navin discussed a deal for Ruth with Barrow at the 1933 World Series. Barrow was anxious to get rid of the aging slugger and urged Babe to meet with Navin and finalize things as soon as possible. At the time, Ruth was about to leave with his family on a long-awaited trip to Hawaii, where he was slated to play in a series of exhibition games. It was a tight schedule—the ship and game reservations were already set—so Babe called Navin and said he would meet him after he returned. It was still nearly five months until spring training, and Ruth figured there would be plenty of time to work things out.

A frustrated Barrow warned Ruth he was making a mistake, but Babe departed for the islands ready for fun and confident of his future. Navin didn't appreciate his action and regarded it as a snub. When Connie Mack began breaking up his latest great Athletics team shortly thereafter, the Tiger owner snatched up Hall of Fame catcher Mickey Cochrane as his new player-manager.

This 1944 Goudy card sports a fine image of the Bambino.

Ruth returned from Hawaii, called Navin, and was politely told the position had now been filled. Detroit would win the pennant the next two seasons under Cochrane, topped off by a world championship in 1935.

"I pulled one of the great boners of my career," Babe admitted in his autobiography. "I don't know if I could have done as well as Mickey, but I would have had pretty much the same material. . . . I can't help but wonder whether those pennants would have gone to me instead of Mickey if I had run out on the first part of my Hawaiian contract."

Barrow had an offer of his own waiting after Babe got the bad news from Navin. Ruth could manage the top Yankees farm club in Newark, New Jersey, thereby getting the experience he needed to handle a big league post. Barrow figured Ruth would jump at the chance, assuming it to be a stepping stone to the Yankees job Barrow never intended to give him. To sweeten the deal, an incentive was even thrown in where a driver would pick Babe up each day from his Riverside Drive apartment and take him to work. Ruth rejected the offer.

"I'm a big leaguer," Babe said, not impressed when Barrow pointed out that Shawkey had also gotten his start at Newark. "Why should I have to go down to the minors first? Cobb and Speaker didn't. Why do I have to? How about that kid in Washington [Cronin, who had become player-manager of the Senators the year before at age 26]? Did he have more experience than me?"

Barrow's response is unknown, but apparently Ruth was still inclined to stick around. He was sent a $25,000 contract for the 1934 season (less than half his '33 pay), and Barrow made sure to release the figures to the press before even Babe knew them. When Ruppert and Ruth met at the brewery for the signing—there was no holdout this time—the Colonel announced to reporters he was "accommodating" Babe's request for a $35,000 salary. The Yanks were probably willing to offer the higher amount all along, but when explained this way the deal left Ruppert looking like a good sport.

The effects of years of hard play were beginning to take their toll on the Babe. Here, the doctor examines a nasty bruise.

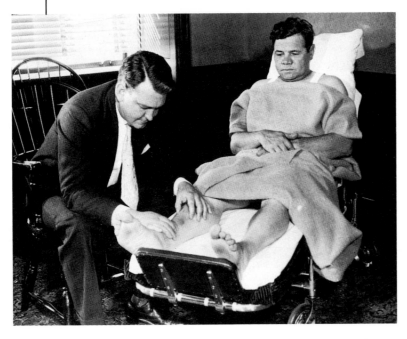

"The management of the Yankees was not discussed," the Colonel said of the negotiations. "McCarthy is still our manager and will remain so for the next two seasons. I have no plans beyond that." Once more there was talk of a managerial spot for Ruth with another club—this time in Cincinnati, where future Yankee executive Larry MacPhail was in charge—but again nothing came of it. Babe would remain in New York at least one more year.

Ruth's salary had been cut $45,000 in three years, but he was still the highest-paid player in the majors. Cochrane was getting $30,000 for his duel duties in Detroit, and Chuck Klein of the Phillies was baseball's only other $30,000 man. Even Gehrig was making just $23,000 for the second straight year, with no cut from Ruppert as his only reward for an outstanding season. All things considered, though, Lou was making about half Ruth's salary but was now twice the ballplayer.

On September 29, 1934, Babe homered against the Washington Senators. As he crossed the plate, as he had done so many times before, a familiar sight awaited him. It would be, however, one of the last times he and Lou Gehrig were in the lineup together.

The previous two years had hinted at it, but the 1934 season truly signified a passing of greatness at Yankee Stadium. Gehrig had the finest year of his career—winning a Triple Crown of his own with a .363 batting average, 49 homers, and 165 RBI while stretching his record playing streak to 1,504 straight games. Despite these fantastic numbers and a great performance from pitcher Lefty Gomez (a league-best 26 wins and 2.33 ERA), the Yankees finished second again, their 94-60 record seven games behind Cochrane's Tigers. Looking for the main cause, fans had to search no further than the man preceding Gehrig in the batting order.

Ruth's demise had accelerated, and his .288 batting average ranked him just fourth among Yankee regulars. In a year when 10 major leaguers hit 25 or more home runs, he managed just 22. There were 19 hitters with over 100

Although this shot left the park, the home runs were coming with less frequency for the Bambino.

RBI, but Babe finished with 84—only the second time he had ever played 100 games and not topped the century mark. The power style he had seemingly singlehandedly ushered in was now in full force, but he was no longer a significant part of it.

He rarely finished games and missed 29 contests completely (including several in May with a bad back). He hit just five homers after July 31. His legs almost completely gone, he was of little help in the field and sluggish on the basepaths. When the Associated Press named its All-Star team following the season, Ruth did not receive a single vote. He was also shut out of the MVP balloting for the second consecutive year. Before the season was over, he was drawing boos at Yankee Stadium. Watching this last event unfold, one reporter wrote respectfully, "tear down Faneuil Hall. Rip up the Constitution. They hooted Babe Ruth yesterday."

After establishing more records than any other hitter over his 15-plus seasons as an outfielder, the only significant mark Ruth helped set in '34 was as the first of Giants screwballer Carl Hubbell's record five straight strikeout victims in the All-Star Game at the Polo Grounds on

After his last game as a Yankee, the Babe towels off and ponders his future.

July 10. For the others (Gehrig, Foxx, Simmons, and Cronin) the event was just a brief failure in the midst of great careers; in Ruth's case it seems, in retrospect, to symbolize how far he had fallen. Had the event occurred a few years earlier, Babe would undoubtedly have been the fifth batter, taken two strikes on purpose—counting them out on his fingers for effect—then swatted a shot into the upper deck.

He became increasingly discouraged as the season progressed, both with his waning skills and the daily reminder in the dugout that McCarthy held the job he felt should be his. Then 10 days following the All-Star Game, he was running to second base when a ground ball by Gehrig hit him on his right shin. He fell quickly to the ground, and while waiting for an ambulance in the clubhouse, he lamented not having taken the day off.

There were a few good moments. He achieved one of his pre-stated goals with his 700th homer on July 13. Fittingly, the 480-foot shot came off Detroit righthander Tommy Bridges in Tiger Stadium—where under different circumstances, Ruth might have been spending all his home games and calling the shots from the dugout. The clout also offered some perspective on Babe's place in the game; at the time he hit it, Lou Gehrig and Rogers Hornsby were the only two other players in baseball with even 300 home runs.

Talk of Ruth's future came up again. Contending that he would never stay in the game as a pinch hitter (a demeaning suggestion Colonel Ruppert had come up with early in the summer), Babe said he would only continue playing if he could also manage. This being the case, it was now generally assumed his playing days were at an end. He was met by large crowds his final time around the league, and nowhere was the reception grander than in Boston.

"Fans Storm Fenway Park In Tribute To Babe Ruth," read the front-page headline in the *Boston Globe*, "Gates Are Closed Early Leaving Fully 15,000 Rooters Milling Outside." The final official count of 46,766 fans for the August 12 game—including several thousand roped off in the outfield—was a record for Fenway, and the crammed masses cheered the Babe throughout a Yankee-Red Sox doubleheader. It was, in fact, the first time Ruth had started both ends of a twinbill all season. Despite his wearing the dreaded New York

Hat on and head down, the Bambino tries to make a quiet exit from Griffith Stadium in Washington after his final outing as a Yank. His young fans, however, still try to get just one more autograph from the Sultan.

uniform, the crowd screamed after each of his two hits (including a double) in the opener and booed Sox pitchers when they walked him twice during the afternoon. They looked the other way when he bobbled Billy Werber's liner to bring in Boston's winning run in the first contest, and the official scorer mercifully ruled Werber's hit a triple.

Twenty years to the month after he first stepped off the train and won his American League pitching debut for the Red Sox on the same field, the returning hero tipped his cap and left midway through the second game to a standing ovation. At this time, most Bostonians probably figured they had seen the last of Ruth the player. They were mistaken. Babe sightings would be a regular occurrence in town the following spring, they just would not be happening at Fenway.

The uniform may be different, but we'd know that swing anywhere. Some exciting touring would follow the end of his term in New York.

The Boston turnout was the final bright spot in a dismal year, and only around 2,000 fans turned out at breezy, overcast Yankee Stadium for the season's final home game on Monday, September 24. No official word it was Ruth's farewell appearance ever came, and after limping down the line following a walk in the first inning, Babe was removed for a pinch runner. There was only thin applause as he left, quite a contrast from the electric presence in the packed yard when he christened it with a home run over 11 years before.

The last contest of the season came six days later in Washington, and the St. Mary's band—perhaps paying Ruth back for his fundraising of 1920—came down from Baltimore to make things a bit brighter for their most famous alumnus and 15,000 onlookers. Ruth was given a testimonial signed by several thousand fans including President Franklin Roosevelt, and the Babe told the crowd over the public address system that he'd like to stay in baseball, "as long as I can do anybody good."

He was hitless in three at bats but did score following a walk. By the eighth inning, Myril Hoag was in right field for the Yankees.

A post-game photo from that day shows a tired, aging Babe smiling wanly and toweling himself off in the clubhouse, but a more telling shot is one of him being quickly whisked through the crowd by policemen as he leaves Griffith Stadium. His hat pulled down nearly over his eyes, looking tired and disillusioned, Ruth appears oblivious to the young kids crowding around him for his autograph. It would seem that the magic was gone.

The discussion of where Babe would be the following season con-

tinued. Before departing to "cover" the World Series for the Christy Walsh syndicate, Ruth went to Ruppert's office looking for an answer. Babe asked just one question: "Are you satisfied with McCarthy as your manager?" Ruppert replied, "Of course I am. Aren't you?" When Ruth said he actually wasn't and thought he could

do a better job himself, there wasn't much more for the two men to discuss. Ruppert said he had no plans to remove McCarthy from his job, and Babe was quickly on his way out the door—this time for good.

The Cards won the Series in seven games, but the biggest story to come out of St. Louis was when Ruth popped off to three New York sportswriters with the official verdict on his future plans. "I'm through with the Yanks. I won't play for them again unless I can manage. But they're sticking with McCarthy, and that lets me out."

A hit in any language! Throngs of avid fans in Tokyo mob the Babe during a parade. This cover of Capper's Farmer *magazine* (left) *still shows the Babe in his New York hat.*

Babe Ruth: His Life and Times

Every news service but the Christy Walsh Syndicate carried the news, and apparently some folks were listening. Impressed by the crowd on hand for Ruth's last game at Fenway (where the Red Sox drew 610,640 all season), Yawkey still wanted

to bring Babe to Boston. Again he was talked out of it by Collins, who knew that Senators owner Clark Griffith was hard up for cash and would take the right offer for Joe Cronin. When Yawkey did just that with an incredible $250,000 offer to Griffith a few weeks later—a record purchase price that dwarfed the cash portion of Babe's sale—Cronin was off for Massachusetts.

This left a managerial position open in Washington, but Ruth was clearly too costly for Griffith. An offer of $15,000 was made, but Babe wanted double that. In the end, the Senators wound up with old friend Harris. While he was still uncertain of his future, Ruth did what came naturally; he had fun. Heading to Japan on a barnstorming tour with an All-America All-Star squad, he was actually getting his first chance to manage as the official field skipper of a team that included Gehrig, Gomez, Foxx, and Gehringer. There would be 22 exhibition games overall, including five in Shanghai and Manila.

Ruth was a hit in the Orient. He rode through the streets of Tokyo in an open car, waving an American flag in one hand and a Japanese flag in the other as thousands roared with delight. Posters adorned with a caricature of the Babe advertised the games, and crowds of up to 80,000 (tickets had been sold out for weeks) packed the two stadiums where the Japanese exhibitions against local pro and college teams were held. Ruth played every inning of every contest (quite a contrast from his American season) and was the leading hitter for both average (over .408) and homers (13) on the trip.

It was 1920 all over again. Ruth clowned with Japanese players and batboys, and in one hilarious photograph was captured trading caps with a youngster whose head couldn't have been much bigger than Babe's nose. He managed to find his way to the geisha houses and golf courses, and when a local newspaper 20 years later ran a poll of the most famous people in Japan the previous four decades, Ruth was the only foreigner to make the list. Memorials honoring his visit would survive long after the war that ravaged the country shortly thereafter.

In his autobiography published six years after Pearl Harbor, Ruth said he had felt genuinely welcomed in Japan. "In my living room on Riverside Drive," he continued in his book, "I still have the large Japanese vases on which are entered my batting exploits of that visit to Japan. But I broke up some of the other souvenirs one Sunday afternoon in December, 1941."

Unbeknownst to Ruth, he was also being watched closely by a member of his own party during the trip. A's owner Connie Mack—then 72 years old—was considering stepping down as his team's manager after 33 years, and by accompanying the American squad to Japan to help run things, he could take a closer look at Babe. Mack had always gotten along well with Ruth, and like other owners knew his presence would help at the gate.

"The Home Run Twins," once very close friends, had not been on speaking terms for some time. As different as two men could be—Gehrig shy, conservative, and tight-fisted; Ruth wild, outgoing, and exorbitant to the point of foolishness with his tipping—they had nonetheless been bridge partners and

This poster from the All-America All-Star tour in Japan sports an unusual caricature of the Babe.

fishing buddies for years. Before their falling out, Gehrig had been in awe of Ruth like everyone else and appreciated the extra money he received as a partner during many of the Babe's barnstorming activities. The fishing and card games were finished, and in time the pair no longer even shook hands when Ruth finished a home run trot with Lou on deck.

The feud caused understandable tension on the Japan trip, as the Gehrig and Ruth families sought to avoid each other at all costs. It also divided the American team into pro-Babe and pro-Lou factions, and Mack noticed. Since it was generally believed the whole mess had been the result of Claire's stubbornness, Mack decided he would be better off continuing to manage himself—which he did for 16 more years before retiring at age 88.

Ruth never knew of Mack's interest and continued enjoying himself. Following the exhibitions in Shanghai and Manila, the team split up, with the Ruths going on to Paris (where Babe lamented his anonymity) and London (where he mastered cricket in one swing). When the S.S. Manhattan docked in New York on February 20, 1935, Ruth was well-rested and ready to find a job. He had a surprise waiting for him.

Judge Emil Fuchs, Babe, and Colonel Ruppert make plans to add another episode in Ruth's baseball life.

The Boston Braves had long been one of the worst organizations in baseball. Shortly after the "Miracle Braves" of 1914 went from last place on July 4 to a pennant and a World Series sweep of Mack's defending champion Athletics, the club had begun a yearly ritual of spending its summers in the second division. Between the years of 1922 and 1932, the Braves had never finished above fifth place or posted a winning record, and their overall winning percentage for the 1920s was .394. The Red Sox (.370) were one of only two clubs to

do worse, lending even more credence to the theory that the sale of Ruth had thrown a curse over Boston baseball.

Yearly attendance at Braves games had fallen as low as 117,478 (the same number as a good week at Yankee Stadium), and even after the fortunes of the club began rising under the guidance of manager Bill McKechnie, the crowds were slow in catching on. A brief run at the pennant and an eventual fourth place finish had attracted a record 517,803 in 1933, but another fourth place showing and the club's best record since 1916 (83-71) drew just 303,205 to cold and cavernous Braves Field the following summer. Part of the trouble was lousy weather, but a more dangerous reason was just a few trolley stops down the road.

Yawkey was spending freely in acquiring the likes of A's pitching great Lefty Grove, the Ferrell brothers (pitcher Wes and catcher Rick), and now Cronin to upgrade the Red Sox and had refurbished cozy Fenway Park into one of the nicest places to watch baseball in the country. The Braves had only one legitimate star in slugger Wally Berger (who held the National League rookie home run record with 38). Their park was a huge, concrete monument to the dead-ball era with center field fences that at one point stood over 500 feet from home plate. Berger had been the only Braves player to ever hit 20 homers in a season there, and fans increasingly grew to favor the long ball action at tiny Fenway.

Cool winds that blew into Braves Field off the Charles River and smoke that drifted in from a rail yard behind left field didn't help matters. The problems of the park were only

Co-owners C.F. Adams and Emil Fuchs sign the slugger with the Braves. After being denied any chance of a managerial position with the Yankees, the Babe sought to pursue his dream with another club.

This book provided one outlet for the Babe's expertise.

201

compounded by ownership woes. The Braves had somehow made money each year from 1930 through '33, but team president and co-owner Judge Emil Fuchs had developed an old Ruthian habit of getting rid of it as fast as it came in. He claimed to have spent $159,000 against a $150,000 profit in '33 alone pursuing new talent, and he still owed as much as $200,000 to minority partners Charles Adams and

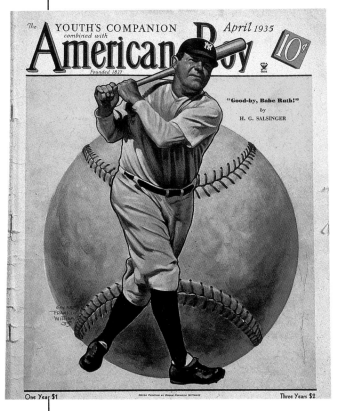

Bruce Wetmore—who had bailed him out of ruin by purchasing substantial amounts of stock back in 1927. He made quite an effort to sell his interest but could find no takers. Just like Frazee a little over a decade before, the judge was in serious trouble.

Shortly before the 1934 National League meetings, Fuchs came up with a plan to bail himself out of debt. Braves Field would be converted into a dog racing facility, and the team would move in with the Red Sox and share Fenway Park. The two clubs had established a good working relationship two decades before, when the Braves borrowed Fenway for the 1914 World Series (their stadium was being built at the time), then returned the favor by offering up Braves Field and its 40,000 seats for both the 1915 and '16 Series. Boston

As this cover of American Boy *illustrates, many New Yorkers would have to bid farewell to the grand slugger.*

teams had won the championship all three times, and everybody appreciated the larger Series shares.

This time things weren't quite so easy. Yawkey was vehemently against the idea—his goal was to make the Red Sox the only Boston team folks wanted to see—and Fuchs's fellow NL owners didn't like the thought of a major league baseball field being overrun by gamblers and greyhounds. The judge eventually gave up his dog dreams. When the owners of Braves Field threatened to evict Fuchs and lease to the Boston Kennel Club, the National League stepped in to guarantee rental on the park and loan Fuchs $7,500 to meet spring training expenses.

His ownership saved for the moment, the Judge soon had another idea. The biggest day in Boston baseball the previous year had been when Ruth came to town, and Boston Mayor James Michael Curley urged the desperate Fuchs to hire the Babe as manager. The Judge refused, saying he was happy with his current arrangement. "I'm committed to McKechnie," Fuchs said. "He's a most satisfactory manager and can stay with me as long as he's in baseball." However, the more the Judge thought about it, the more he liked the idea of Babe Ruth in a Braves uniform.

Now a Boston Brave, the Bambino meets with two Native Americans in D.C.

There were some snags. Babe had stated he would never sign another player contract unless he could also manage, and Ruppert had said he would never release him to play for another team. Barrow simply wanted Ruth gone for good, and so he worked out a plan that would make everybody happy. "I'm ready to make an offer for Ruth," Fuchs said in Boston after the scheme had been devised. "We will make him assistant manager and give him an official position if he comes to the club, and he can play as often as he likes."

Nobody bothered to ask then what an assistant manager was or did, but Babe suddenly seemed interested in playing baseball again. Talking with reporters the day the Manhattan docked in New York, he spoke mysteriously of "having something under consideration that I can't talk about right now. . . . All I can say is, it has to do with big league baseball."

The fish was hooked. The next day Ruth spoke to Ruppert to get a further understanding of the Braves offer, then telephoned Fuchs for final details. As Fuchs explained it to him, Babe would be a vice president of the Braves, sharing in organizational profits, and with a first option to buy club stock. He would also be assistant manager to McKechnie, and in a year or perhaps earlier would take over as manager when Bill moved up to general manager. Babe would be a regular player when he felt able and a pinch hitter the rest of the time. His base pay would be $25,000—more than anyone on the team including McKechnie.

Everything was put down in a lovely letter the judge sent to Ruth the following day, a letter that gave new meaning to the term "double-speak" and, in effect, promised Babe nothing but a straight player contract. The letter Fuchs sent follows.

Mr. George H. Ruth, New York, N.Y.   February 23, 1935

My Dear George:

In order that we may have a complete understanding, I am putting in the form of a letter the situation affecting our long-distance conversation of yesterday.

The Boston Braves offer you the following inducements, under the terms and conditions herein set forth, in order to have you sign a uniform contract plus an additional contract which will further protect you, both contracts to be filed.

1. The Boston club offers you a straight salary contract.
2. They offer you an official executive position as an officer of the corporation.
3. The Boston club offers you also the position, for 1935, of assistant manager.
4. They offer you a share of the profits during the term of this contract.
5. They offer you an option to purchase, at a reasonable figure, some of the stock of the club.
6. The details of the amounts agreed upon will be the basis of a separate contract which shall be a personal one between you and the club, and, as the case may be, with the individual officials and stockholders of the club.

In consideration of this offer, the Boston club naturally will expect you to do everything in your power for the welfare and interest of the club and will expect that you will endeavor to play in the games whenever possible, as well as carry out the duties above specified.

May I also give you the picture as I see it, which, in my opinion, will terminate to the best and mutual interest of all concerned.

You have been a great asset to all baseball, especially to the American League, but nowhere in the land are you more admired than in the territory of New England that has always claimed you as its own and where you started your career to fame.

The fans of New England have a great deal of affection for you, and from my personal experience with them are the most appreciative men and women in America, providing, of course, that you keep faith, continue your generous cooperation in helping civically and being a source of consolation to the children, as well as to the needy, who look up to you as a shining example of what the great athletes and public figures of America should be.

I say frankly, from my experience of forty years interest in baseball, that your greatest value to a ball club would be your personal appearance on the field, and particularly your participation in the active playing of exhibition games, on the ball field in championship games, as well as the master-minding and psychology of the game, in which you would participate as assistant manager.

As a player, I have observed and admired your baseball intelligence, for during your entire career I have never seen you make a wrong play or throw a ball to the wrong base, which leads us to your ability to manage a major league baseball club. In this respect we both are fortunate in having so great a character as Bill McKechnie, our present manager of the club, who has given so much to baseball and whom I count among my closest friends. Bill McKechnie's entire desire would be for the success of the Braves, especially financially, as he is one of the most unselfish, devoted friends that a man can have.

That spirit of McKechnie's is entirely returned by me, and I know by my colleagues in the ball club. They feel, as I do, that nothing would ever be done until we have amply rewarded Manager McKechnie for his loyalty, his ability and sincerity, which means this, George, that is it was determined, after your affiliation with the ball club in 1935, that it was for the mutual interest of the club for you to take up the active management on the field, there would be absolutely no handicap in having you so appointed.

It may be that you will want to devote your future years to becoming an owner or part owner of a major league ball club. It may be that you may discover that what the people are really looking forward to and appreciate in you is the color and activity that you give to the game by virtue of your hitting and playing and that you would rather have someone else, accustomed to the hardships and drudgery of managing a ballclub, continue that task.

So that if we could enter into the spirit of that agreement, such understanding might go on indefinitely, always having in mind that we owe a duty to the public of New England that I have personally learned to love for its sense of fairness and loyalty, and it is also in this spirit that I hope we may be able to jot down a few figures of record that will prove satisfactory to all concerned.

Sincerely yours,

Emil E. Fuchs, President

Ruth never showed this monstrosity to a lawyer, nor did he pick up on its subtle loopholes. After asking Ruppert one more time if McCarthy was the best man to manage the Yankees (the colonel assured him he was), Ruth decided to take the offer. He and Ruppert went to Boston to finalize things with Fuchs, then the three met with the New York press the next day to talk sweetly of each other and make the deal official. Speaking of how they had "always been friends," Ruppert handed Babe a piece of paper on which were 16 words that set Ruth on the path to oblivion: "Mr. George H. Ruth: You are hereby notified as follows: 1. That you are unconditionally released. (Signed) Jacob Ruppert."

Babe later said in his auto-biography that the process of having a 15-year relationship with the Yankees severed in such a staged manner "made me a little sick," but on this day there were nothing but smiles all around. Ruth paused when he was asked what his role would be as vice president, and Fuchs chimed in by saying

Dizzy Dean watches the Babe warm up in his new uniform.

he would be "consulted on trades and so forth." The Colonel couldn't help getting in a little dig of his own. "A vice president signs checks," he spouted, and the room erupted with laughter. Reached in Boston, a suddenly supportive Tom Yawkey predicted the move would be "of great benefit to a great baseball city—one which surely can support two baseball teams and support them well."

It was just six days since Ruth had returned from his trip. While he was sad to be leaving New York, he had every reason to believe his new position in Boston was the beginning of a great new career that would prove as successful—and profitable—as the first. Asked if he and McKechnie might have a rocky relationship, the Babe said, "I'm sure we'll get along lovely," before breaking into more talk of his own pending managerial career.

There was more doublespeak from Fuchs at a huge Boston dinner in Babe's honor a few days later. All of this verbal runaround did little to deter the Babe's enthusiasm over his multi-roles, but then came a rather ominous reply from McKechnie: "The Babe would help any ball club. But I'm interested in him only as a player. He wouldn't be worth a plug nickel to us if he didn't get into uniform and go up there to bat." When one *Boston Globe* headline read rather prematurely "Babe Ruth to Manage Braves in 1936," McKechnie had a simple answer for that as well: "That's news to me."

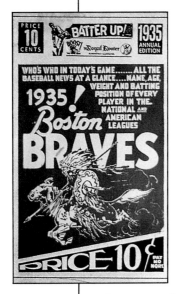

It was now 21 years since a Baltimore train had brought the big 19-year-old youth into Back Bay Station. Now, George Herman Ruth was returning to Boston.

There had been no winter workouts at Artie McGovern's gym, and Ruth reported to spring training in St. Petersburg (and 3,000 frenzied fans at the train station) weighing 245 pounds and in poor shape. Photographs from his first days with the Braves show his stomach sticking out as if someone has stuck a medicine ball under his sweatshirt, and after a while someone realized it would be wiser if Babe kept his uniform on at all times. The uniform itself, white with red trim and the large Braves' logo in the center, looked strange after so many years in regal pinstripes. The team didn't even have a new one big enough for him, and Ruth had to make due with an ill-fitting hand-me-down from robust catcher Shanty Hogan.

You can't tell the players without a scorecard. For the first time in 1936, the Babe would no longer be listed as a Yankee but as a member of the Boston Braves.

Just as his first days with the Yankees had brought new life to New York's spring training, Ruth drew huge crowds and media attention wherever he went with the Braves. A March 16 battle with his former club in St. Petersburg was played before the largest gathering of fans ever to see an exhibition in Florida. The Babe, however, hit no homers then or at any time the first month of camp. The revitalization seen in Japan had been a false sign; Ruth didn't belong in the outfield and wasn't producing at the plate. McKechnie used him at first base in place of holdout Baxter Jordan. He didn't look much better there, but at least he didn't have to run.

"Rabbit" Maranville and new teammate Ruth mug it up for the camera.

This group represents members of the 1935 Braves who were also former Yankees.

Even Ruth later admitted his performance was frustrating: "The kids were striking me out or making me pop up. . . . It was a rotten feeling." About the only fun he had other than talking about his pending managerial position was bumming around with the club's 43-year-old shortstop Walter "Rabbit" Maranville, a 5'5", 155-pound pixie who matched Ruth's appetite for adventure and was also nearing the end of the line. On a club of mostly journeymen, the two old-time stars could relate to one another.

Relating to McKechnie was another story. The manager was getting sick of all the attention the Babe was getting—especially since Ruth kept yakking about taking over his position. Besides, Bill had no idea where he was going to put the Babe once Jordan signed. When somebody asked McKechnie for the umpteenth time what Babe's leadership role on the team would be, he snapped back, "Ruth's title as assistant manager means nothing particularly."

Babe showed a little life with three exhibition homers as the club headed north. He was starting in left (Baxter had signed) when Boston opened the regular season against the Giants at Braves Field April 16. It was Babe's first time playing there since he had pitched the

Somehow, it just doesn't seem right to see the Babe without his pinstripes.

Red Sox to a 2-1, 14-inning victory over Brooklyn in the 1916 World Series, and 22,000 fans, including five New England governors (the largest Opening Day crowd

Babe Ruth: His Life and Times

The Bambino had more time to wonder about his future and what it might bring.

Although he didn't get into as many games as he used to, the Babe could still provide rough and tumble action when necessary.

in the park's history), braved 39 degree temperatures to see if he could rise to the occasion again. On the mound for New York was his old chum Carl Hubbell—he of the five consecutive All-Star strikeouts. Hubbell was coming off a 21-12 season and was arguably baseball's best pitcher. When the portly 40-year-old Ruth stepped to the plate with one runner on in the first inning, it looked like a pure mismatch.

It was. Ruth lined a single to right to drive in Boston's first run, then scored its second a few moments later. The score was still 2-0 when Hubbell came to the plate in the top of the fifth with a man on, and when he lined a shot to left, Babe made a great one-hand catch while running past the foul line. Babe was up again with a man on in the bottom of the inning. This time he smashed a Hubbell screwball into the right field bleachers for his first NL homer and a 4-0 lead. Boston claimed a 4-2 victory, and Ruth echoed the thoughts of many when he said of the performance, "I didn't dream I'd ever get off to such a start."

The city went nuts, especially when Ruth added two more hits in the second game. The Braves were going all the way, folks surmised, and the Babe was going to lead them there. It was great newspaper copy, but it was also pure fantasy. Ruth was in no condition to be a savior, and this was no championship club. Berger was a fabulous slugger (especially considering his home park's dimensions), but other than him there were no legitimate stars. It was a mediocre club at best, and distractions caused by Babe's presence made

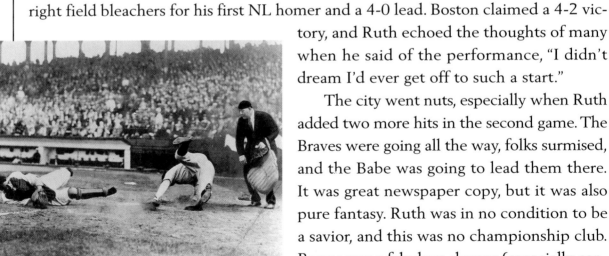

it difficult for McKechnie to maintain control and seemed to affect the team's on-field play.

Bill didn't know it, but he wouldn't have to worry about the distraction for long. In the next month Ruth had just two more hits (one of them a homer against the Dodgers on Easter Sunday), and his average fell well below .200. He missed several games with a cold and various other ills. The club had already settled deep into the second division by this point, and the few fans who came to Braves Field booed unmercifully as reality set in.

Babe's profit sharing situation wasn't looking very good, and neither was his supposed leadership role on the club. As a vice president he seemed to hold no duty more important than that of a greeter and front office puppet. An increasingly perturbed McKechnie sought no advice from his "assistant manager" as the team wallowed near the cellar. Soon the whole scheme became apparent to Ruth; McKechnie wasn't going to be moving up to general manager, and he wasn't going to be taking Bill's place. The entire

contract and Fuch's letter had all been a public relations scam.

The realization was unsettling for the Babe. He had given the major leagues over 20 years of his life, saved baseball from extinction following its greatest scandal, and was now being denied a chance to stay in the game on his own terms. For the greatest hero in American sports history, it didn't seem a fitting epilogue.

As reality set in, the Babe knew his days as a player were coming to a close. One can only imagine the hurt the big guy suffered.

1935-1948

The Sultan Steps Down:
Long Live the King

"A man who has put away his baseball togs after an eventful life in the game must live on his memories, some good, some bad."

—Babe Ruth, from
The Babe Ruth Story

THE SULTAN STEPS DOWN: LONG LIVE THE KING

Previous page:
Everyone's favorite son,
the Babe tips his hat to
the hometown crowd.

The view from the room in which Babe Ruth was born looks out on the exterior of Oriole Park at Camden Yards, home to the Baltimore Orioles since 1992. This seems appropriate; Babe broke in with Baltimore when it was a minor league club. Center field in the new park lies atop the foundation for a bar George Ruth Sr. owned while his son was away at St. Mary's. In the restaurants and pubs surrounding the inner harbor area where restless young Babe roamed, pictures of the city's most famous athletic alumnus still grace the walls.

Such memories, however, are not confined to archaeological digs and old photos. In the months leading up to Ruth's 100th birthday celebration, Baltimore began preparing for a party the likes of which the city had seldom seen. There would be the groundbreaking for a bronze statue of Ruth at Camden Yards, a rededication of

his birthplace, an exhibit of 40 artistic works depicting Babe in clay, paint, and photographs. Of course, what would a celebration for the Babe be without plenty of hot dogs, pop, and beer for everyone. More visitors were expected at the Babe Ruth Birthplace and Baseball Center than at any time since its 1974 opening.

Why all the fuss? It's true that Babe Ruth was a ballplayer without peer, but that was only part of it. He was all things innocent, wild, and free, a man of huge charisma and charm so endearing that three cities—Baltimore, New York, and Boston—claim him as

In the closing chapter
of his career, the Babe
still possessed the stance
that had become as
legendary as his
other attributes.

their native son. He was given credit for saving baseball when he emerged as a star in New York following the "Black Sox" scandal, and in the wake of a continuing Major League strike he was getting people excited about the game all over again— more than 45 years after his death.

"One of my favorite stories comes from a man who went to the first Cooperstown induction ceremony in 1939 when he was 11 years old," said Greg Schwallenberg, curator of the Babe Ruth Birthplace. "Babe came over to a group of kids right in the middle of the ceremony and just started handing them quarters. They did not care about getting his autograph; they just wanted to meet him. None of the other players even noticed them, but he went out of his way. That's just who he was."

Ruth's move to the Braves in 1935 failed to revitalize his career. His performance continued to decline at the plate and in the outfield, and he was now enduring the added indignity of playing on a horrible team before sparse, cynical crowds for an owner who was knowingly exploiting him. He had expected to become Boston manager within a year, but no matter how poorly the club did

Tired and near the end of his distinguished lifetime in baseball, the Babe pauses thoughtfully on the Braves bench.

it was becoming obvious Bill McKechnie was keeping that job. Babe's titles of vice president and assistant manager meant nothing, and there were even reports in the papers of teammates resenting his big salary. For a man who held the affection of others above almost everything, this must have been hard to take.

The results were inevitable. Embittered and embarrassed, Ruth failed to appear at various promotional functions. One merchant, upset by a snub at his store, returned 500 unsold tickets to Fuchs. Soon Babe and the Judge were feuding openly. "You attend to your end of the business, and I'll attend to mine," Ruth said during one such fight. "Mine is on the field." Unfortunately, his argument didn't really hold much weight; whatever his business on the field was supposed to have been, Babe knew he wasn't living up to it. His age, weight, and legs wouldn't let him.

"He couldn't turn, you see?" recalled Wally Berger, who played alongside Ruth in center field. "He'd go in pretty good to field a ball, but he couldn't turn on those damn knees and ankles. So that made my job no easier. Every time there was a ball hit out toward Babe, I'd be out there to back him up."

The man who had carried teams to championships was now counting on others to carry him. He just couldn't cope with that. On May 12 Ruth told Fuchs and McKechnie he wished to be put on the voluntarily retired list—a move meaning he could remain Braves property while not being on the active roster. Babe's goal was to hang onto his titles and keep his managerial chances alive.

Babe called a conference to meet with the press. Although his news was sad to share, he couldn't take any more of Judge Fuchs and empty promises.

The Judge would have no part of it. His eye on the till at all times, Fuchs convinced the humbled hero to stay on as a player at least through the club's upcoming western road trip, where ticket sales and profits were expected to be strong. Babe made some comments about quitting that made the papers but agreed to go on the trip. "I'd be mighty sorry if he retired," said the sweet-talking Fuchs. "Perhaps this trip will restore his peace of mind."

At first it didn't. The club played woefully in St. Louis and Chicago, and Ruth's average fell to .155 amidst complaints of watering eyes and a persistent cold. He homered and made a pair of fine catches against the Cubs on May 21, then moved on with the team to Pittsburgh. He managed just one single over the first two games at spacious Forbes Field but sent right fielder Paul Waner to the wall with three deep drives that would have been home runs in any other park. Perhaps his swing was finally starting to come around.

The finale of the Pirates series was Saturday, May 25. Facing lefty Red Lucas in the first inning, Babe hit a two-run homer into the lower right-field grandstands. Former Cubs bench jockey Guy Bush was pitching when Ruth came up again in the third, and the result was the same—a two-run homer, this time into the upper grandstands. A third at bat in the fifth produced a run-scoring single, and Bush was still on the mound in the seventh when Ruth came to the plate a final time.

Connecting on a curve ball, Babe sent a drive fifty feet over the double-deck roof in right field and completely out of the park, marking the first time the feat had been accomplished at Forbes Field. It was only the second time Ruth had ever hit three homers in a game, and Bush tipped his hat to his old rival as Babe limped around the bases. "I never saw a ball hit so hard before or since," Bush said afterward. The Babe still could swing the lumber.

It was his 714th—and last—major league home run. Despite this brief respite, his physical condition was winning out. His wife Claire, Braves' traveling secretary and former teammate Duffy Lewis, and others urged Ruth to quit then and there, but muttering something along the lines of "I can't, I promised that . . . I'd finish all the towns on this trip," he plodded on. Cincinnati brought three strikeouts the first day and a trio of hitless games, and he struck out twice and walked twice in the first contest at Philadelphia May 29. Both cities had welcomed his arrival with Babe Ruth Days.

On May 30, in the first game of a Memorial Day doubleheader against the Phillies, Babe hurt his knee going after a fly ball in the first inning. He left the game, watched the Braves get swept, and never played in the majors again. Fuchs had grown increasingly frustrated and desperate—he was losing more money each

The Babe lived his life like a legend, doing everything on a grand scale. He lived big and played hard. It should come as no surprise that his exploits and accomplishments not only inspired tributes in many forms throughout his playing days but still do even today.

month and had borrowed against his Braves stock—and he and Ruth were at it again. The Judge yelled at Babe for not appearing in a doubleheader at Boston the following afternoon (he claimed his knee hurt too much), but the final straw came when Ruth asked for a few days off to go to New York and a swanky reception aboard the luxury ocean liner Normandie. He figured his injury would keep him from playing against the Dodgers in the following series anyway, so what was the harm?

The King wields his scepter. Now a private citizen, the Babe finds himself surrounded by a wealth of memories.

"Nothing doing!" said the Judge. "You stay here." Babe supposedly offered to suit up for an exhibition game scheduled in Haverhill, Massachusetts, the next afternoon before leaving, but Fuchs wouldn't budge. The pressure point for both had been reached, and in the middle of that afternoon's game against the Giants, Ruth sent word to the pressbox he had something important to tell reporters right then and there.

"I hate to say what I'm going to say," Ruth told writers hastily gathered in the Braves' clubhouse. "I'm not quitting, but I'm going on the voluntary retired list. That means I can't play for at least 60 days anyway. I want it understood that I don't want to get out of baseball. If Judge Fuchs were to sever connections with the Braves, I'd gladly come back. But I won't have anything to do with the club as long as Judge Fuchs has."

Reaction was mostly as expected. McKechnie said he was sorry to see Ruth go and denied having ever mentioned anything about Babe breaking training rules or other team regulations. Braves players swamped their teammate for autographs when he told them of his plans before the game, and Fuchs gave him his unconditional release while making the ridiculous claim, "I did everything I could to help him along, but I guess it wasn't to be."

Ruth and his family left the very next morning for the drive back to New York. McKechnie came to see them off, and Babe later said this proved the manager had not felt ill will toward him. If McKechnie did believe Ruth was disrupting the ballclub, it was soon obvious they were no better off without him. The Braves were 10-27 and in last place as Babe drove away and wound up 38-115—the worst record by any National League team during the 20th century. They not only finished 61½ games out of first place, they were 26 games out of seventh. Just how bad were they? Even with his .181 batting average and only 71 at bats, Ruth's six home runs ranked second on the club.

If there was any consolation for Babe, it came in July—when Fuchs was forced at last to sell out to Charles Adams. A little over a year later the Judge officially declared bankruptcy.

In spite of his optimistic tone in the Boston press conference, Ruth was not to return to major league baseball in 60 days or ever again as a player. Even with a bad reputation among his fellow owners as a near-bankrupt bumbler, Fuchs still had the support of his brethren when it came to evaluating player attitude. If the Judge said Babe was a bad soldier, then a bad soldier he was—and not somebody they wanted in their organization. It was the old boy network in full force, and Babe was the victim.

As it became apparent he wasn't going to play again, Babe still held out hopes for a managerial post. He had been shut out by Barrow and Ruppert, erred in judgement with Navin of Detroit, and come close to getting jobs in Philadelphia and Boston. Surely there would be more chances, and this time he would be ready and willing.

The offers never came.

"It was the biggest disappointment of his life—no question about it," Babe's daughter Julia Ruth Stevens

Now this would make an interesting game! The Bambino had his share of words with umpires. He certainly seems the figure of authority.

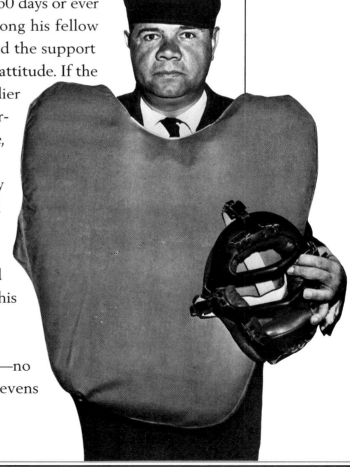

said 60 years after the Braves fiasco. "He felt even if he didn't make good—and he was sure that he would—he should have been given the chance. That's what hurt him the most."

Proudly, Ruth said during the 1935 World Series that if owners didn't give him his shot by the winter meetings in December, "I'll look outside baseball for a job."

Just as his last salary demands failed to move Barrow and Colonel Ruppert, the threat caused not even a stir. Just like that, Babe was out of the game.

He did the same things many ex-ballplayers do. He bowled, he hunted (where his great eyes made him a crack shot), and with an average in the high 70s, pondered a career as a professional golfer. One thing he did not do much of was go to baseball games. His request for Yankee Stadium passes may or may not have been turned down by Barrow (another tale passed down through the years), but Babe always claimed he was told by one Stadium operator he would have to send in a check for tickets to the 1936 opener at "The House that Ruth Built."

The Babe stands by daughter Julia on her wedding day. Just three years earlier, he had rushed to her side when it was discovered they had the same blood type. The Babe was glad to donate a pint to help her heal.

Spurned by the game, the domestic life he had been settling into during the last years of his career now became more of a priority. As his daughters grew older, Ruth became a stereotypical overprotective father—examining dates and enforcing a midnight curfew. When Julia was suffering from a severe strep throat in 1938 and needed a blood transfusion, Babe hurried home from an exhibition game in Albany to supply what was needed once it was discovered he had the same blood type

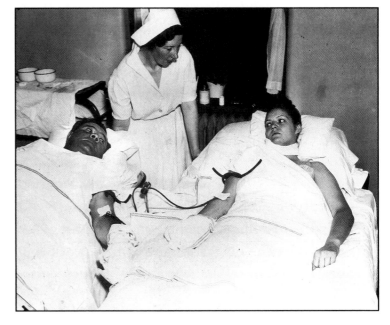

as his adopted daughter. Julia recovered soon thereafter, and Babe was there to walk her down the aisle at her wedding three years later. He looked quite dapper in black tails and a top hat.

Living comfortably on the money Claire had carefully saved and the new cash still coming in from endorsements, the Ruth's maintained the same core group of friends from the old days and had frequent visitors to their Riverside Drive apartment. They played cards, hosted parties (including one each year on Babe's birthday), or Claire simply read aloud to her husband—a habit she had picked up when Ruth was still with the Yankees and didn't want to strain his eyes. He enjoyed beating his mother-in-law at checkers, and if Julia and her friends needed a fourth for bridge Babe was always accommodating. He never missed an episode of his favorite radio programs—especially *The Lone Ranger* and *Gangbusters*.

Golf filled much of the Babe's schedule these days. An overzealous crowd at this charity tournament brought the game to an early close as they jammed the gallery area and proceeded to pick up his shots as souvenirs.

Golf was now his main athletic release. He was a very strong player who once beat future U.S. and British amateur champion Dick Chapman in a tournament, but erratic drives and a weak putting game curtailed his dreams of a pro career. He was forever working at his game, however, and trips to the St. Alban's course on Long Island (with a stop at the butcher's along the way for steaks to eat later in the clubhouse) became a regular part of his routine.

It was a seemingly happy time. Babe was a cheerful, humorous player, able to poke fun at the shortcomings of his own game and always capable of drawing a crowd. When he participated in a New York charity match with famous athlete Babe Didrikson Zaharias and two others, it drew a gallery of 12,000. Play had to be stopped when crowds rushed the fairways each time Ruth prepared to shoot.

It was a comfortable life, but it lacked the adventure and challenge he had previously enjoyed. He would drive by spring training sites on his winter jaunts to Florida and playfully yell, "Hiya, slaves!" to the ballplayers, but in reality he longed to be one of them. He often seemed discontent and depressed in his early years of retirement, and Claire later wrote of the period, "Oh, how I hated baseball and everything in it in those days."

One acknowledgment he had not been completely cast aside came in 1936, when Ruth was one of the original five inductees into the still-uncompleted National Baseball Hall of Fame in Cooperstown, New York. A total of 226 sportswriters voted from a list of 10 for those players they felt most deserving the honor, with 170 votes needed for election. The final tally: Ty Cobb 222, Babe Ruth and Honus Wagner 215 each, Christy Mathewson 205, and Walter Johnson 189. His archrival Cobb had barely beaten him out, but Ruth still had the distinction of being the youngest of the original inductees.

Babe filled his leisure time with many activities. He enjoyed taking hunting trips, like this one in Nova Scotia.

On one of his rare trips to the park with Claire, Babe drew the usual crowds and autograph hounds for a June 15, 1938, game at Brooklyn. Ruth wasn't the real story that night; the Dodgers-Reds contest was the first major league night game in New York City, and Cincinnati's Johnny Vander Meer chose the occasion to pitch his second consecutive no-hitter. Dodgers executive Larry MacPhail, however, noticed the attention the Ruths received. He had first thought of signing Babe while with the Reds three years before, and now the thought crossed his mind again. Brooklyn was in a three-way battle for baseball supremacy in New York; maybe Ruth's drawing power could put the Dodgers over the top.

MacPhail approached Babe with a $15,000 contract to serve as first base coach. Once again, Ruth naively saw the offer as a stepping stone to bigger things. The

Dodgers were a mediocre ballclub, and manager Burleigh Grimes apparently knew it was his final year. MacPhail had brash veteran shortstop and team captain Leo Durocher (another Ruth nemesis from the Yankees days) in mind as a replacement, and even stated openly that Ruth was not a candidate for the post. Anxious for any chance to be back in the game, Babe took the job anyway.

"Babe Ruth belongs in baseball," MacPhail told the press, but just as in Boston, Babe was not given any major responsibility. His job was simply to be a gate attraction. He was to take batting practice, play in exhibitions, and stand at first base smiling. Looking more well-rounded than ever in his stark white uniform, the 240-pounder handled these "duties" well and had soon won over everyone on the team with his clubhouse banter and storytelling on the bench (except Durocher). Attendance improved dramatically, and when he starting shooting balls into the seats during warm-ups, 43-year-old Ruth began pondering a comeback.

The process of becoming an active player again was as simple as tearing up his coach's contract and signing a new one, but Grimes was against it. "He's 43 and he can't see," said the 45-year-old former 20-game winner. "If he can hit, I can still pitch." Grimes threw batting practice for the Dodgers himself, but Ruth couldn't even handle his stuff. He warmed up instead with the soft serves of former catcher Merv Shea. Grimes feared Babe might get injured by an inside fastball were he to appear in a real game.

Ruth kept on coaching. Grimes obliged MacPhail by going over signs and occasionally his pitching choices with the Babe. The fans couldn't get enough of the big guy. Babe spent an hour or more signing autographs outside Ebbets Field after games and always made sure even the smallest kids in the back row went away happy. When the Dodgers returned to Braves Field, Ruth made a fan for life out of 13-year-old clubhouse boy (and future traveling secretary) Donald Davidson when he asked, "Hey kid, you like to play catch?"

Fans in Brooklyn loved seeing the big guy. They were especially thrilled when he'd step up to the plate before the game and crank one out of the park.

Durocher was not quite as enamored of the big fellow. His old contempt for Ruth—who had snubbed Leo when he was a cocky rookie with the '27 Yankees—surfaced regularly. Ruth never bothered learning the signs Grimes showed him; whether he found it difficult or unnecessary is unknown. He never needed them as a player and didn't intend to start now.

Grimes usually handled such duties for Brooklyn anyway while coaching at third, but one day a young writer erroneously reported that Ruth had given the Dodgers a 1-0 victory by calling for a successful hit-and-run play in the eleventh inning. Grimes (who had called the play himself) yelled at the reporter for the mistake, and Durocher used it as an excuse to taunt Babe in the clubhouse. The two scuffled briefly before Grimes pulled them apart, and Ruth wound up with a mark under his eye.

The riff between Babe and Lou would eventually heal. Their falling out, though, supposedly kept Babe from getting one managerial post.

MacPhail heard about the fight second-hand, and if he had ever given consideration to Ruth as more than a gate attraction, his mind was set now for good. At year's end, he found a way to let him depart with dignity. There wasn't enough room for both Durocher and him on a seventh place team anyway, and when Leo was given the manager's job three days after Grimes's October 10 firing, a reporter asked about Ruth's status. "Ruth was never considered by us for the post as manager," said MacPhail. "He could have remained with us as a coach, but he told me that he would not be available."

Once again, Babe Ruth was out of work. The talk of his trouble with signals had clinched it; there would be no more big league chances for the Babe. He was left now to golf, bowl, and hunt; to live comfortably on his own terms; and to occasionally serve as a showpiece for baseball. He may or may not have "waited by the phone" for a managerial chance to come, but he always held out hope. He was still under 45, but all around him the people and things he had known were changing.

Then, in January 1939, Colonel Ruppert died. Ruth went to see him in the hospital and was moved when Ruppert whispered, "Babe, Babe" during the visit. It was the first time he hadn't called him "Root" during their long and often tumultuous relationship, and Babe left the dying man's room in tears.

Lou Gehrig was also dying, although for a while nobody knew it. After what was considered a "down" year in '38 (.295, 29 homers, 114 RBI), 35-year-old Lou had stumbled through the start of the 1939 season batting .143. A trip to the Mayo Clinic determined that he was barely able to get around on the ball or handle routine grounders at first. He was suffering from amyotrophic lateral sclerosis, a rare and incurable nerve disease that would later bear his name.

Gehrig's consecutive game streak ended at 2,130 when he pulled himself from the lineup on May 2; he was never to play again. "Lou Gehrig Day" was held at Yankee Stadium on July 4, and a packed house turned out to pay homage to the noble hero. There were plenty of wet eyes during Gehrig's moving speech, which concluded, "I might have had a tough break, but I have an awful lot to live for." Ruth, too, was terribly moved by Lou's speech. The Babe went over to shake his old friend's hand but wound up impulsively hugging him instead—ending the long and petty feud between them. It was the first time Gehrig smiled all day. As they embraced, a tearful Babe couldn't have imagined he would be facing a similar crowd under very similar circumstances less than a decade later.

On Lou Gehrig Day, the two former teammates put aside any hard feelings. After Lou gave his farewell speech, the Bambino gave him a hug. It was the only time Lou smiled all day.

The Pride of the Yankees *is the story of Lou Gehrig's life. The Babe plays the part of himself in this fine film.*

This shot was taken during the making of the Pride of the Yankees. *Babe has a cup of java with Gary Cooper, who portrayed Lou Gehrig*

Gehrig died in June 1941, and that fall Ruth was invited to play himself in *Pride of the Yankees*—a film telling the story of Lou's life in baseball. Although he weighed close to 270 pounds and had suffered a pair of mild heart attacks in the past two years, Babe was determined to make a strong and realistic performance. Putting himself on a strenuous diet, he shed over 45 pounds before filming started in early '42.

His portrayal was so realistic, in fact, it got him in a little trouble. During one scene the Yankees are shown celebrating yet another pennant with some playful wrestling on a train, and when Ruth put his hand through a Pullman car window during the melee, he suffered severe cuts that required stitching. He also battled pneumonia during the filming and wound up back in the hospital for two weeks. Rumors circulated that he was dying (even doctors claimed he was "fighting for his life"), but he soon recovered and was out playing golf by April.

Ruth and Cobb face off on a different field of green.

"USO deserves the support of every individual citizen."

Ruth did more for the World War II effort than bust up his Japanese souvenirs on Pearl Harbor Day. That same summer of '41, he came up with the idea of teaming with old rival Ty Cobb in a best-of-three golf match—the proceeds naturally going to war charities. Playing before large crowds in Boston, on Long Island, and in Detroit, the duo raised plenty of dough as well as their own competitive juices. Cobb eventually won two of the three matches.

Babe generated even more revenue with volunteer work on behalf of the Red Cross and bought an additional $100,000 worth of war bonds himself.

In 1943, Giants slugger Mel Ott was the teammate as he and Ruth went on the air with WABC radio in New York, "batting out" $25 and $100 war bonds to fans willing to lay down cash to talk to the greatest home run hitters in American and

National League history. Babe also visited four or five military hospitals a week, and in an act almost impossible to fathom today, appeared onstage at New York movie matinees in the summer of '43, urging audiences to contribute salvageable material to the war cause.

Of all his acts of kindness during this period, none pleased the Babe more than his 1942 "duel" with Walter Johnson, Washington's great fireballing Hall of Famer who had gone 417-279 in his major league career but just 3-6 in pitching matchups with Ruth. The two agreed to face each other again (Babe batting this time) between

Walter Johnson serves some up to the Bambino in 1942. The Babe sent two over the fences.

games of an August 23 doubleheader at Yankee Stadium. While waiting to be announced, the two had a humorous exchange. "Babe, I just want to ask one thing; don't hit any back to me," Johnson asked. "Hell, I'll be lucky to hit one at all," Ruth answered with a laugh. "But I'll try to pull 'em down the line."

As 69,000 fans cheered on, the 47-year-old slugger came through twice—first hitting a line drive into the lower right field stands on his third swing and then connecting on the 20th pitch for a huge smash into the third deck in right; as he rounded the bases and hugged Johnson at home plate, nobody seemed to care that the ball

Babe Ruth and Tony Galento are flanked by radio stars Bud Abbott and Lou Costello at this charity function. The four donned Santa suits to get in the spirit of things.

had hooked foul at the last moment. He appeared in two more charity contests at the Stadium that summer. He would appear in no more formal games. His hair turning gray, Ruth said to one New York writer in the summer of '44, "It's hell to grow old." Still, he was magic. When *Esquire* magazine ran a poll to name the greatest living sports personality that year, Ruth outdistanced runner-up Joe Louis 4-1.

After yet another hospital stay to remove knee cartilage (which he playfully inspected with a forceps for the benefit of photographers), a stint as a wrestling referee, and a brief fling in Mexico City (being wined and dined by promoters of the doomed Mexican League), Ruth got his futile managerial hopes up a final time following the war. The Yankees were sold by the Ruppert estate to a syndicate headed by MacPhail. Babe phoned his old friend in the fall of 1946 offering to manage the Yankees or even the Newark farm team—a job he had proudly turned down as being beneath him a decade before.

MacPhail said he would get back to him, and about a month later a letter came. "They write the bad news and telephone the good," Ruth said to Claire. He was right. Explaining that former Yankees catcher Bill Dickey would be taking the Newark job, MacPhail went on to add: "While I cannot recommend your appointment as manager of the Yankees I believe there is a place in baseball on a basis which should be acceptable to you. . . . There is an important job to be done in the Metropolitan New York area in connection with the promotion and development of sandlot and amateur baseball."

It was a final, powerful message. Ruth loved kids and would do anything for them. When you're inquiring about a major league managerial job, however, being offered a similar post with nine-year-olds is downright insulting. "Babe walked into the kitchen, numb," Claire later wrote of her husband's latest and last snub. "It was the same kitchen where he had sat before on a chair, head in hands, and wept in fury and frustration. He wept once again."

Ruth's next medical emergency occurred around the same time. All through the summer of '46 he had a severe pain over his left eye. What was at first thought to be a toothache or sinus infection eventually caused so much discomfort he was admitted to a New York hospital on November 26. The entire left side of his face was swollen, his left eye was closed, and he was unable to eat solid food. Doctors removed three bad teeth, then administered penicillin and other drugs. A month later, though, Ruth was still in pain and still in the hospital.

"They weren't really sure at first what it was, so they kept trying all kinds of different things—and none of them worked," said Julia Ruth Stevens. "When they did figure it out, they never told daddy, they never told mother, and they never told me—but we had our suspicions."

Claire and the Babe visit during one of his stays at the hospital.

What he had was cancer. Doctors finally discovered that a malignant growth had formed around the major artery in the left side of his neck. In the operation that followed, nerves were cut and the artery tied off. It was determined that the disease had originated in the naso-pharynx, a part of the air passage behind the nose that was unapproachable by surgery. Not all the cancer could be removed. Claire said she was eventually told the situation later, but Babe remained in the dark (at least as far as others knew) until the end.

The surgery was on January 5. In the month that followed, Babe remained confined to the hospital in a state of near constant pain and depression. His hair began to fall out, he lost a lot of weight (between 80 to 128 pounds), and expected to die.

Telegrams from the likes of Connie Mack and Jack Dempsey poured in. Claire read to him from these and some of the thousands of letters that arrived each week. One seventh-grader from New Jersey sent a religious medal and the moving message, "I know this will be your 61 homer. You will hit it." Babe wore the medal pinned to his pajamas the rest of his life. On February 6, he celebrated his 52nd birthday in the hospital with Claire, Julia, and their dog, Pal, and they listened to a recorded greeting from Eddie Collins and Ted Williams. As the outpouring of support continued (including four birthday cakes), Babe's spirits improved.

Although no one ever officially told him, the Babe must have known his health wasn't improving. News of his condition sparked concern and put him back on the cover of several publications.

On February 15, Ruth was released from the hospital and wept upon seeing the hundreds of admirers gathered outside as he was led to a waiting car. The traditional camel's hair overcoat and cap couldn't hide the obvious; it was feared time was running out. Baseball commissioner A.B. "Happy" Chandler declared April 27 would be "Babe Ruth Day" at Yankee Stadium and every other park in the league. Even in war-torn Japan (where footsoldiers had supposedly been taught to yell "The Hell with Babe Ruth!" when on the attack) there were monetary rewards for every homer hit that afternoon in honor of the great "Beibu Rusu."

Time has a tendency of altering history. Many fans and amateur film-makers believe April 27, 1947, was Babe Ruth's last appearance at Yankee Stadium. It wasn't, but since he looked so poorly and the words he spoke in his cracking, hoarse voice have been re-played so many times, it has become known as his farewell speech. It may as well be; although his posture was stooped and he was shaky, his eyes tired and drawn, and his hair grayer than ever, he was eloquent and sincere in his message.

Yankees manager Bucky Harris chats with Babe in the New York dugout.

"Thank you very much, ladies and gentlemen," he began after a long coughing spell. "You know how bad my voice sounds. Well, it feels just as bad." He continued, "The only real game in the world, I think, is baseball." Babe spoke of the need for children to begin playing at age six or seven. "You've got to let it grow up with you, and if you're successful and you try hard enough, you're bound to come out on top, just like these boys have come to the top now."

He had a tip of the cap and a smile at the speech's end for the crowd of 58,000 (thousands more had listened over loudspeakers in other parks), but Julia remembered him feeling awful throughout the afternoon. The remaining piece of the tumor was growing, and morphine was necessary to stop the discomfort. Babe still tried to

Babe makes his farewell speech at Yankee Stadium on April 27, 1947.

live his normal life of golf outings and steaks, but now the drives fell far short off the tee and the meat was chopped up for him. Soon even biting down on the white of an egg caused excruciating pain.

Treatment with an experimental drug beginning in late June improved Ruth's health tremendously. Soon he had gained back much of his weight and was traveling 50,000 miles around the country as a representative for the Ford Motor Company and American Legion youth baseball. It was to be only a momentary reprieve. The pain returned that fall, and when read today, the optimistic closing to his autobiography *The Babe Ruth Story* (written with old friend Bob Considine that hopeful summer of '47) seems almost eerie:

"I've got to stick around a long, long time," it reads. "For above everything else, I want to be a part of and help the development of the greatest game God ever saw fit to let men invent—Baseball."

Ruth attended the Dodgers-Yankees World Series that fall and in December dressed up as Santa Claus to entertain young polio victims. More messages of his mortality were forthcoming, though. By the end of the year Brother Gilbert was dead of a cerebral hemorrhage, and Walter Johnson had succumbed to a brain tumor. Babe may not have known or wanted to believe it, but his own time was growing short.

Babe went to Florida for spring training in '48 and met with Joe McCarthy, Ted Williams, and others, but he looked worse than ever. He said he felt 90 years old on his 53rd birthday; he was soon back in New York. His next major trip was to Hollywood, where he was billed as the technical advisor for the film version of *The Babe Ruth Story*, then being rushed through production to beat the inevitable. The Ruths wound up never seeing any of the scenes being filmed, and the Babe's "advising" consisted of posing for pictures showing star William Bendix how to hold a bat. It was just as well; Bendix obviously wasn't a very good student, and the picture was a cliché-ridden travesty.

Ted Williams, slugger for the Boston Red Sox, gets a few words of advice from the master.

On Sunday, June 6, a tanned and emaciated Ruth gave a copy of the completed manuscript for *The Babe Ruth Story* to Yale University baseball captain George Bush, who couldn't foresee that photographs of the moment would be used during his successful presidential campaign 40 years later. A celebration honoring the 25th anniversary of Yankee Stadium was scheduled for the following Sunday. The Babe attended despite cold, rainy weather that left him with a constant chill throughout the day.

He entered the locker room after his old teammates, who watched in hushed silence as he was slowly helped into some clean, fresh pinstripes. There were photographs and smiles by his old locker (which, like his number three, had not been used since his retirement). The Bambino then waited with a coat draped over his shoulders in the runway while the rest of the oldtimers were introduced. Finally his name was announced over the loudspeakers, and as

Future president George Bush (in Yale uniform) receives a copy of the manuscript for The Babe Ruth Story *from the Babe. The movie, unfortunately, was poorly executed and does not do justice to the Bambino's career.*

The Babe suits up for one last time. In honor of his accomplishments, his number and locker have not been used since his retirement.

The House that Ruth Built. Resting on his bat for support, he spoke to the admiring crowd on the 25th anniversary of Yankee Stadium.

W.C. Heinz so aptly wrote, "He walked out into the cauldron of sound he must have known better than any other man."

The words Ruth mumbled to the crowd that day have been forgotten, but one photograph of the event has endured as perhaps the most poignant in sports history. Taken from the back, it shows Babe standing at home plate, photographers and former teammates off to the side, while in the distance a crowd roars and the championship pennants his heroics produced flutter in the chilly afternoon wind. His cap is off and in his left hand, while his right hand rests on his bat—now a means of support rather than a weapon.

On July 26, the Ruth's went to the New York premiere of *The Babe Ruth Story*, but as Julia remembered, "he was so sick and so medicated that I'm not even sure he knew where he was." Babe and Claire left shortly after the picture started, and he never ventured from Memorial Hospital again. Answering letters and meeting with visitors right up until August 15, he died in his sleep at 8:01 P.M. the following evening. His last conscious act was reportedly autographing a copy of his autobiography for one of his nurses. News of his death hit the papers and air waves immediately, and for the first time the words "throat cancer" were publicly linked to his name.

A long line of mourners encircled Yankee Stadium to pay their respects as Ruth's body lay in state.

Over a two-day period, more than 100,000 passed his open casket inside the ballpark. They were men, women, and children of all races and ages; from Little Leaguers dressed in uniform to old gentlemen in derbys whose rooting interest in baseball pre-dated the 20th century. Vendors sold hot dogs and photographs of the Babe to those waiting their turn.

Another 75,000 were on hand for his funeral at St. Patrick's Cathedral (most of them standing in the rain outside), and Cardinal Spellman delivered the mass in a service befitting an esteemed head of state. The only larger funeral in Ruth's lifetime had been that of President Franklin Roosevelt three years before. For someone

On June 13, 1948, Babe spoke to a packed house at Yankee Stadium.

As a final tribute to the Sultan, fans line the path along Fifth Avenue in New York as the funeral cortege makes its way to St. Patrick's Cathedral.

who in his own unorthodox way had touched so many, it seemed an appropriate send-off.

"It was absolutely amazing, and I've heard a lot of different stories about it," said Julia Ruth Stevens of the last crowds her father drew. "One man told me he had taken his little boy, who he had to carry, to Yankee Stadium during the viewing. He said when his son grew up, he wanted to be able to tell him he had seen Babe Ruth."

According to Bill Guilfoile, vice-president of the National Baseball Hall of Fame, the most popular attraction in the entire Cooperstown museum is the life-size wooden sculpture of Babe Ruth that stands just inside the main entrance. Younger kids often have no idea who the strange-looking fellow in pinstripes is, but they stand by nonetheless as parents shoot their picture alongside the Sultan of Swat. By the time these same youngsters pass by the statue on their way out, they've usually become Ruth fans themselves.

This photo captures just a small segment of the 100,000 people who came to pay their last respects to the greatest player of all time.

Now, 100 years after his birth and 60 years following his final game, the magical appeal of Ruth is as strong as ever—even if some of the facts surrounding his career have been skewed. For many under the age of 65, their only image of the Babe is in the movie portrayals by William Bendix (1948) and John Goodman (1993), performances that have helped alter history and portrayed the graceful slugger otherwise. Ruth did not hit three home runs in his last game and then quit on the spot as Hollywood would have us think, nor did he require the aid of pinch-runners to complete his home-run trots. He didn't sport a pot belly until late in his career and began his career not as a slugger—but as a great pitcher.

It may be wrong for folks to believe such things, but tell them the truth and they don't really care. Because it's the Babe, they want to believe it all. The Babe Ruth Museum ran a poll a few years ago in which visitors were asked to vote on whether or not Ruth called his home run off Charlie Root in the 1932 World Series. Despite equal evidence to support both claims—and perhaps even a shred more disproving the feat—a full 97 percent of voters believed the homer had been called.

In Canada, too.

WHEATIES

"Breakfast of Champions"

"Champions get many a small boy to eat a good breakfast!"

Betty Crocker

Young or old, big or small, everyone loved the Babe.

Even in bad films the point seems clear—this was a ballplayer and man worshipped like none other. Everywhere he went, people seemed to be smiling. His jovial, moon-shaped face was used to endorse everything from cereal to chewing tobacco to razors to underwear (yes, Babe Ruth's All-American Athletic Underwear), and more than 15 songs were penned in tribute to the Maharajah of Mash—among them Irving Berlin's "Along Came Ruth" and the forgettable 1948 post-mortem ditty "Safe at Home." The latter reads in part: "He was called out, here below, but he's safe up there I know."

There have been several literary treatments of the story, from the autobiography published just before Babe's death to the host of historical tomes that emerged just as Henry Aaron was approaching and passing his career home run record in 1974. "What attracted so many people to Ruth?" H.G. Salsinger wrote shortly after Babe's death. "He was rowdy, rough, tough, profane, ribald, swaggering. He had most of the human faults and weaknesses, but he also had most of the human virtues and probably the greatest of them were honesty, complete unselfishness, charity and love for his fellowman. Ruth never pretended to be anything but what he was."

Roger Maris and Mickey Mantle pose with Claire Ruth in 1961. That year, the hitters attempted to break the Babe's record of 60 homers.

The phenomenon continues today. Named the greatest major league player of all time in 1969 by the Commissioner's Office (the same year his birthplace was saved from the wrecking ball by a group of Baltimore businesspeople), Ruth was one of the first three celebrities—James Dean and Elvis Presley were the others—taken on posthumously in 1982 as clients for the Curtis Management licensing firm. Thanks to the Babe's popularity, the company has since added nearly 200 clients ranging from Lou Gehrig to Malcolm X.

This powerful legacy has at times been a curse to more contemporary players. Babe's standards for most home runs in a season (60) and a career (714) have been eclipsed by Roger Maris and Henry Aaron, respectively, but the fact that both these record-breakers received tremendous media and public pressure from a ghost, his relatives, and thousands of fans during their chase is testimony to the Babe's staying power. Claire Ruth was asked for comment each time someone got close to one mark or the other. She was the first to point out that Maris had eight more games to get his 61 homers and Aaron nearly 4,000 additional at bats to get his 755.

Even with the handicap of less playing time, Ruth stands up well against the all-time statistical leaders. In addition to being second to Aaron in both homers and RBI (2,211), he is tied with Aaron and behind only Cobb in runs (2,174). His .342 batting average ranks him 10th. No one can match his .690 slugging average, 2,056 walks, 11 home run titles, and ratio of hitting 8½ home runs per every 100 at bats. He trails only Reggie Jackson with his 15 homers and .744 slugging mark in the World Series, but if there is one statistic that proves Ruth was the greatest of them all, it is this—he was also 94-46 with a 2.28 ERA as a pitcher. When baseball historian Bill James unveiled his new formula for evaluating player performance, Ruth came out as the most valuable player in baseball history. Nobody else was close.

It's true; technically he is no longer the home run king. Even the Babe himself said all records are meant to be broken. Everyone agrees, however, that he was truly amazing. Babe Ruth—a kid at heart with a smile that spread from ear to ear. You can almost see him standing at home plate, grinning and giving a wink right before he sends a shot out of the park. Long live the King!

Farewell, Bambino.
We'll never forget you.